SHEPHERD'S NOTES

SHEPHERD'S NOTES

When you need a guide through the Scriptures

Proverbs

Nashville, Tennessee

Shepherds Notes—*Proverbs*
© 1998 Broadman & Holman Publishers, Nashville, Tennessee
All rights reserved
Printed in the United States of America

ISBN# 0-8054-9016-7

Dewey Decimal Classification: 223.707
Subject Heading: BIBLE. O.T. PROVERBS
Library of Congress Card Catalog Number: 98-27116

Library of Congress Cataloging-in-Publication Data
Garrett, Duane A.,
         Proverbs / Duane Garrett A., editor [i.e. author].
              p.   cm. — (Shepherd's notes)
         Includes bibliographical references.
         ISBN 0-8054-9016-7 (trade paper.)
              1. Bible.   O.T.   Proverbs —Study and teaching.   I. Title.
         II. Series
         BS1467.G37   1998
         223'.707—dc21   98-27116
                                                                            CIP

1 2 3 4 5 6   03 02 01 00 99 98

CONTENTS

FOREWORD

Dear Reader:

Shepherd's Notes are designed to give you a quick, step-by-step overview of every book of the Bible. They are not meant to be substitutes for the biblical text; rather, they are study guides intended to help you explore the wisdom of Scripture in personal or group study and to apply that wisdom successfully in your own life.

Shepherd's Notes guide you through the main themes of each book of the Bible and illuminate fascinating details through appropriate commentary and reference notes. Historical and cultural background information brings the Bible into sharper focus.

Six different icons, used throughout the series, call your attention to historical-cultural information, Old Testament and New Testament references, word pictures, unit summaries, and personal application for everyday life.

Whether you are a novice or a veteran at Bible study, I believe you will find *Shepherd's Notes* a resource that will take you to a new level in your mining and applying the riches of Scripture.

In Him,

David R. Shepherd
Editor-in-Chief

DESIGNED FOR THE BUSY USER

Shepherd's Notes for Proverbs is designed to provide an easy-to-use tool for getting a quick handle on these significant Bible books, important features, and for gaining an understanding of their messages. Information available in more difficult-to-use reference works has been incorporated into the *Shepherd's Notes* format. This brings you the benefits of many advanced and expensive works packed into one small volume.

Shepherd's Notes are for laymen, pastors, teachers, small-group leaders and participants, as well as the classroom student. Enrich your personal study or quiet time. Shorten your class or small-group preparation time as you gain valuable insights into the truths of God's Word that you can pass along to your students or group members.

DESIGNED FOR QUICK ACCESS

Bible students with time constraints will especially appreciate the timesaving features built into the *Shepherd's Notes*. All features are intended to aid a quick and concise encounter with the heart of the messages of Proverbs.

Concise Commentary. Short sections provide quick "snapshots" of the themes of these books, highlighting important points and other information.

Outlined Text. Comprehensive outlines cover the entire text of Proverbs. This is a valuable feature for following each book's flow, allowing for a quick, easy way to locate a particular passage.

Shepherd's Notes. These summary statements or capsule thoughts appear at the close of every key section of the narratives. While functioning in part as a quick summary, they also deliver the essence of the message presented in the sections which they cover.

Icons. Various icons in the margin highlight recurring themes in the books of Proverbs, aiding in selective searching or tracing of those themes.

Sidebars and Charts. These specially selected features provide additional background information to your study or preparation. Charts offer a quick overview of important subjects. Sidebars include definitions as well as cultural, historical, and biblical insights.

Questions to Guide Your Study. These thought-provoking questions and discussion starters are designed to encourage interaction with the truth and principles of God's Word.

DESIGNED TO WORK FOR YOU

Personal Study. Using the *Shepherd's Notes* with a passage of Scripture can enlighten your study and take it to a new level. At your fingertips is information that would require searching several volumes to find. In addition, many points of application occur throughout the volume, contributing to personal growth.

Teaching. Outlines frame the text of Proverbs, providing a logical presentation of their messages. Capsule thoughts designated as "Shepherd's Notes" provide summary statements for presenting the essence of key points and events. Application icons point out personal application of the messages of the books. Historical Context icons indicate where cultural and historical background information is supplied.

Group Study. Shepherd's Notes can be an excellent companion volume to use for gaining a quick but accurate understanding of the messages of Proverbs. Each group member can benefit from having his or her own copy. The *Note's* format accommodates the study of themes throughout Proverbs. Leaders may use its flexible features to prepare for group sessions or use them during group sessions. Questions to guide your study can spark discussion of Proverbs's key points and truths to be discovered in these delightful books.

LIST OF MARGIN ICONS USED IN PROVERBS

Shepherd's Notes. Placed at the end of each section, a capsule statement provides the reader with the essence of the message of that section.

Historical Context. To indicate historical information—historical, biographical, cultural—and provide insight on the understanding or interpretation of a passage.

Old Testament Reference. Used when the writer refers to Old Testament passages or when Old Testament passages illuminate a text.

New Testament Reference. Used when the writer refers to New Testament passages that are either fulfilled prophecy, an antitype of an Old Testament type, or a New Testament text which in some other way illuminates the passages under discussion.

Personal Application. Used when the text provides a personal or universal application of truth.

Word Picture. Indicates that the meaning of a specific word or phrase is illustrated so as to shed light on it.

THE FUNCTION AND BACKGROUND OF PROVERBS

In the Bible, Proverbs is the primary example of wisdom literature. Although the definition of "wisdom" is subject to debate, the main idea behind biblical wisdom is fairly clear. It teaches how we should live in the day-to-day existence of this world. That is, instead of dealing with the covenant, creation, prophecy, or even specifically God's requirements as laid down in the Law, wisdom deals with the marketplace, the law courts, domestic relationships, and social order.

This is not to say that Proverbs cares little about morality. Far from it: Morality and the fear of God are the foundation of everything in biblical wisdom. But the purpose here is different from what one finds, for example, in Deuteronomy or Isaiah. In those books, the central points are that the Lord is the covenant God of Israel and that Israel must obey the terms of His covenant. But the point of Proverbs could be summarized like this: *Here is how you ought to live if you want to be successful and prudent, have a good family life, get along with your neighbors, be a responsible citizen, and in general find happiness.* Thus, Proverbs gives great emphasis to the fact that a young man should avoid prostitutes not so much because going to them violates the covenant with God (although this is true) but because going to prostitutes is self-destructive.

Throughout the book, the reader is addressed as "my son." This term implies that biblical wisdom literature arose in an environment of parents teaching their sons, and it also tells us that Proverbs regards the family as the primary arena for moral development.

The voice of Proverbs is that of parents appealing to their sons to do the right thing. In ancient Israel, men were the leaders of their households and of society. It is perhaps for this reason that Proverbs gives so much emphasis to the training of the young man. Although anyone can read and profit from Proverbs, it is clearly meant primarily for boys who are coming of age and must make some basic decisions about what path they will follow in life. The book frequently warns boys about entering gangs, engaging in violent crime, going to prostitutes, and marrying nagging women. The fundamental idea behind Proverbs is that if the young men go bad or make poor decisions, their families and all of society will be in chaos.

AUTHORSHIP AND STRUCTURE OF PROVERBS

Proverbs 1:1 tells us that these are the proverbs of Solomon. Although many scholars today regard the connection between Solomon and wisdom literature to be fictitious, there is no solid reason for taking so skeptical a position. To the contrary, it is reasonable to suppose that the age of Solomon was the heyday of Israelite literary accomplishments. In the ancient world, wisdom literature was highly regarded, and as a general rule there is a great literary flowering at the same time that a culture reaches great political and economic power. In Greece, the era of great dramatic literature emerged after Athens had won victory over the Persian Empire and became the dominant power of the eastern Mediterranean. Rome had its great literary flowering in the age of Augustus. If Israel really did reach its economic and military summit under Solomon, it would be surprising if it did not produce its greatest wisdom literature at this time.

Actually, however, it is not quite correct to speak of the book of Proverbs *as we have it today* as written by Solomon, at least not in the sense we might understand it. Proverbs is actually made up of four major collections of material followed by an anonymous poem. The first collection is Solomon's book of instruction (Prov. 1–24). The second is a series of Solomonic proverbs that were collected and presumably edited by the scribes under Hezekiah (Prov. 25–29). The third is the collection by Agur (Prov. 30), and the fourth is the collection of Lemuel (31:1–9). The poem is the song of the good wife in 31:10–31. Thus, the book as we know it today did not come into existence until the reign of Hezekiah (who lived more than two hundred years after Solomon), but a substantial amount of the text is Solomonic.

THE MATERIAL OF PROVERBS

Proverbs expresses its teaching in many ways. Most people know about the "proverb," a short saying, that gives the book its name. Actually, however, Proverbs does not move into giving individual proverbs until chapter 10; in chapters 1–9 we see, instead, long discourses. These are, for the most part, of two kinds. The first is the "parental appeal," in which the father (or mother) exhorts, urges, and pleads with the son to do what is right. The second is the "wisdom appeal," in which wisdom, personified as a woman, calls for the young man to come to her and learn her ways.

The book also contains a wide variety of proverbs. Some proverbs directly command the reader, and some merely describe a truth. Some proverbs are called "better sayings" because they declare that one condition is better than another (e.g., Prov. 16:8). Some are called "numerical sayings" because they use an ascending numerical pattern to make a point. An example is in Proverbs 30:18: "There are three things that are too amazing for me, four that I do not understand." The "wisdom poem" is a poem or song

The arrangement of this material follows the normal patterns of ancient wisdom literature. In the Near East, wisdom literature basically followed one of two forms. The simpler form was a text that merely gave a title (usually with some reference to who wrote or compiled it) followed by the main body of instruction. The Hezekiah, Agur, and Lemuel collections are all of this kind. Each begins with a short title (25:1; 30:1; 31:1) and then moves directly into its teaching. The other form is more complex; it has a title, a prologue, and then the main body of teaching. Within this main body, however, there may be several subtitles and subdivisions. The collection of Solomon is like this; it has a title (1:1) and a prologue (1:2–7), and then it divides its main body of teaching with several subtitles (e.g., at 10:1).

that teaches some lesson of wisdom; 31:10–31 is an example.

It is also important to know that proverbs are often collected in groups. Sometimes these proverb groups deal with a single theme, such as laziness. Sometimes they follow certain patterns. For example, four proverbs might deal with two different topics, but arrange them as follows:

A: First proverb on topic one

    B: First proverb on topic two

A´: Second proverb on topic one

    B´: Second proverb on topic two

This kind of arrangement is called "parallelism" because the first pair (A and B) parallels the second pair (A´ and B´). A second common arrangement is to have the second group repeat the topics of the first group, but in reverse order. For example:

A: First proverb on topic one

    B: First proverb on topic two

    B´: Second proverb on topic two

A´: Second proverb on topic one

Chiasmus is a way of arranging a text so that the second half parallels the first half, but does so in reverse order. For example, if the first half has three parts: A, B, and C, the second half will have three parallel parts in reverse order: C´, B´, and A´. Wisdom texts from the ancient world frequently made use of chiasmus. In a chiasmus, the central element is often the most important part of all.

This is called "chiasmus." A third pattern is to have a group of proverbs that are bracketed by a pair of similar proverbs on either end of the collection, like a pair of bookends. For example:

A: First proverb on topic one

(Various proverbs on various topics)

A´: Second proverb on topic one

These patterns can become quite complex and involved, but they are helpful because they give proverbs context and order. Also, the same proverb can be used several times in different places but with a different emphasis because it is set in several collections that focus on different topics.

THE OUTLINE OF PROVERBS

As described above, the book of Proverbs is made up of four major collections with a wisdom poem appended at the end. Within these collections, one sees an enormous variety of detail, much of it too complex and involving units too small to lay out in a brief outline. Nevertheless, the larger units of text are clear, as follows:

I. The Collection of Solomon (1:1–24:34)
  A. Title (1:1)
  B. Prologue (1:2–7)
  C. Discourses (1:8–9:18)
  D. Subtitle (10:1)
  E. Proverbs (10:2–22:16)
  F. Subtitle (22:17)
  G. Thirty Sayings (22:18–24:22)
  H. Subtitle (24:23)
  I. Short Discourses (24:24–34)
II. The Collection of Hezekiah (25:1–29:27)
  A. Title (25:1)
  B. Main Text (25:2–29:27)
III. The Book of Agur (30:1–33)
  A. Title (30:1)
  B. Main Text (30:2–33)
IV. The Book of Lemuel (31:1–9)
  A. Title (31:1)
  B. Main Text (31:2–9)
V. In Praise of the Good Wife (31:10–31)

The word translated *proverb* literally means "saying." The Hebrew word can refer to all kinds of sayings, slogans, or proverbs, but here it refers especially to the kind of short, moral maxim that we call a "proverb."

In the ancient world, a wise man was supposed to be adept at all kinds of intellectual activities. This included first of all the ability to give moral direction, to solve intellectual problems (including "riddles"), and to present ideas in a pleasing, clear way. Second, a wise man was supposed to be able to interpret omens from the gods. In this regard, Joseph and Daniel were superior to their contemporaries because they could interpret difficult dreams and signs (Gen. 41; Dan. 2; 5).

TITLE AND PROLOGUE (1:1–7)

As indicated in the introduction, this is the title of the first "book" of Proverbs, 1:1–24:34.

Proverbs promises the reader that those who study this book can become wise in the first way but makes no such promise about attaining the second kind of wisdom—the ability to interpret omens—probably because this was a special gift of God. This text tells us about a kind of wisdom that is available to all. This wisdom is *practical*, because it helps us deal with the daily problems of life. This is so-called common sense of a "prudent life." Second, this kind of wisdom is moral and involves "discipline" and "discernment." Third, this wisdom is *intellectual* in that it involves solving "riddles" and "parables."

Verse 7 separates biblical wisdom from all other forms of wisdom and instruction. It asserts that the "fear of the Lord" is the foundation of all true wisdom. This does not mean that people outside the faith have no wisdom, or indeed that those within the faith are all wise. It means that the whole quest for wisdom is vain if one misses the fundamental truth, which is God. Those who desire to be wise should first orient themselves toward God and then all other, lesser truths will fall into place. Also, this verse introduces us to the principal dichotomy of this book, the way of the wise and the way of the fool. Throughout proverbs, we see the contrast between the way of the wise (morality, integrity, and the fear of God) and the way of the fool (self-indulgence, deceit, and selfishness).

■ *Proverbs aims to teach the ordinary person*
■ *how to be wise. This does not mean all of us*
■ *will have the spectacular insights of a Joseph,*
■ *but we can all live a prudent and upright life,*
■ *and we can also become people with active,*
■ *inquisitive minds. The basis for all true wis-*
■ *dom, however, is the fear of God.*

QUESTIONS TO GUIDE YOUR STUDY

1. What type of literature is Proverbs?
2. For whom were many of the proverbs originally collected?
3. What four collections of sayings appear in Proverbs?
4. What is parallelism?
5. What is chiasmus?

PROVERBS 1:8–5:23

- - - -

FIRST PARENTAL EXHORTATION (1:8–19)

The book opens with an exhortation to the young man to stay out of trouble. He faces peer pressure to join a gang and temptation to go after easy money. The text opens with a general appeal to listen to parental instruction (vv. 8, 9). Verse 10 summarizes the message: stay out of gangs! In verses 11–14, we have the offer that the gang makes: "Join us, and you will be part of the group and have plenty of easy money!" The gang also promises to be as ferocious and irresistible as death itself (v. 12). It seems that modern gangs are not the first to be fascinated with images of death.

In verses 15–19, we learn what really happens to those who follow this path. The violence they rush into comes back upon them. Verse 17, as it is rendered in most versions, makes little sense. It seems to say that birds recognize a trap when they see a net being spread out. Apart from the fact that this is doubtful, it has no clear relevance to the context. A better translation is, "In the eyes of a bird, the net is strewn with grain for no reason." In other words, a bird sees someone lay out a net and spread grain over it but cannot see the connection between the two actions. When the bird flies down to eat the grain, he is caught.

In the same way, the gang members do not see the connection between their violent way of life and the early deaths that befall their members. They simply chase the promise of easy money down to their own graves.

- ■ *Proverbs opens with an appeal for the young*
- ■ *man to avoid the trap of gangs and violence.*
- ■ *The first temptation the book describes is the*
- ■ *temptation to crime and quick money. Later,*
- ■ *the book will deal with the temptation to*
- ■ *easy sexual gratification.*

FIRST WISDOM APPEAL (1:20–33)

A: Introductory appeal for listeners (vv. 20, 21)
  B: Address to fools (v. 22)
    C: Missed opportunity (v. 23)
      D: Reason for announcement
      (vv. 24, 25)
        E: Judgment (vv. 26–28)
      D´: Reason for announcement
      (vv. 29, 30)
    C´: Certain Punishment (v. 31)
  B´: Destiny of fools (v. 32)
A´: Appeal for someone to listen (v. 33)

Wisdom here is personified as a woman who calls out for young men to come to her. She is the counterpart to the prostitute, who also seeks for young men in the streets (Prov. 7). We need to bear in mind that Lady Wisdom here is a personification. She is not a goddess. Her going out and calling to men symbolizes the fact that wisdom is available to all. People have every opportunity to learn the right way; but they choose to ignore the call of wisdom.

The entire emphasis of this text is on the fate of those who ignore wisdom. Almost nothing is said of the benefits of wisdom. Probably the text focuses on the negative for rhetorical purposes; it is easier to get people to pay attention with warnings of disaster than with promises of a good and wholesome life. Also, the primary function of wisdom is to keep us out of the path of self-destruction.

Wisdom herself cannot promise eternal life, but she can keep us from ruining our lives.

■ *Wisdom, personified as a woman, appeals*
■ *for men to learn from her by warning them of*
■ *the disaster they face if they ignore her. She*
■ *gives her first speech in a chiastic form in*
■ *which the central element—calamities that*
■ *will befall fools (1:26–28)—is the main*
■ *point of the text.*

SECOND PARENTAL EXHORTATION (2:1–22)

Although it is true that life is made up of many little decisions, each of which shapes us in some way, it is also necessary to make some big decisions that will guide us in dealing with smaller issues. In particular, one must decide whether to follow the path of righteousness and submission to God.

One of the fundamental doctrines of Proverbs is the "two ways." This is the fact that each person must choose either the life of integrity and the fear of God or the life of selfishness and disdain for God's ways. On the surface, this approach seems overly simple. Many people have high moral standards in one area but are woefully deficient in another area. Some Christians fail to live exemplary lives, and some unbelievers live by a high moral code. Nevertheless, Proverbs deals in generalizations, and it is a valid generalization to say that one must decide whether to follow a personal ethic governed by the fear of God or by self-interest.

All of verses 1–4 is an extended *if* clause (the "protasis"), and all of verses 5–11 is an extended *then* clause (the "apodosis"). In other words, verses 1–11 make a single statement: Here are the benefits for choosing to go in the right way. Following the right way is here described as submitting to wisdom. Verses 1–4 use three images to get across this point. First, one should be like an attentive student listening to a teacher (vv. 1, 2). Second, one should plead for wisdom like a person who pleads for a gift from a king (v. 3).

Third, one should seek for wisdom as eagerly as one would dig for a buried treasure (v. 4).

In verses 5–11, the text describes two benefits that come from seeking wisdom. First, one will be able to see that God truly delivers those who trust Him. Verses 7, 8 could be translated as follows: "He will treasure up success for the upright. He will be a shield for those who walk in integrity, for the one who keeps the paths of justice." Second, according to verses 9–11, those who seek wisdom will have the moral insight necessary to avoid the snares of sin and immorality.

In verses 12–19, we read of the two tempters who seek to draw the young man from the right path. These are the wicked man, who seeks to draw the young man into crime (vv. 12–15), and the immoral woman, who seeks to draw him into promiscuity (vv. 16–19). The first offers him easy money and the second offers him easy sex. Both use twisted arguments and seductive words to draw him away, and both lead him to the grave.

Verses 20–22 conclude with a summary statement to the effect that those who follow the right way will live but those who turn aside will die. Proverbs rarely deals directly with the covenant between God and Israel because it focuses more on general truths, but the emphasis here on remaining "in the land" is similar to the teaching of Deuteronomy (cp. Deut. 5:16, 31, 33).

■ *Everyone must decide whether to seek wis-*
■ *dom or to seek easy money and easy sex. The*
■ *decision is somewhat deceptive since it seems*
■ *to involve choosing a hard, disciplined life*
■ *over against a life of fun and ease. In fact, it*
■ *is a choice between life and death.*

THIRD PARENTAL EXHORTATION (3:1–35)

Although we can rightly call this chapter as a whole a "Parental Exhortation," it is also a very complex set of smaller exhortations. The outline of this chapter is as follows:

    I. Opening Parental Appeal (vv. 1–4)

    II. A Call for a Devout Life (vv. 5–12)

    III. A Hymn to Wisdom (vv. 13–18)

    IV. Wisdom in Creation (vv. 19, 20)

    V. Second Parental Appeal (vv. 21–26)

    VI. On Being a Neighbor (vv. 27–30)

    VII. On Criminal Behavior (vv. 31–35).

To bind wisdom to the neck is not just to have an adornment; the neck (literally "throat") was the seat of life in Hebrew thinking. To have wisdom about one's neck and in one's heart is to have one's identity molded by wisdom.

Some people believe that Proverbs endorses a somewhat facile notion that those who are righteous will automatically be blessed with health and wealth. This seems to find support in verse 2, which asserts that following the teachings of wisdom will give long life and prosperity. In fact, Proverbs never teaches that righteousness is the path to riches. It does, however, proclaim the general truth that those who live prudent and devout lives will escape the pitfalls that bring people to poverty or an early grave. Furthermore, verse 3 tells us that our goal should be to have our inner character transformed by the word of God.

Verses 5–12, the call for a devout life, is divided into three parts. True piety shows itself in intellectual humility (vv. 5–8), in how one uses material wealth (vv. 9, 10), and in patient acceptance of God's discipline (vv. 11, 12). The first of these three (vv. 5–8) reminds us not to seek to find truth without first submitting to God. This is not an anti-intellectual spirit that flees hard questions and does shoddy research. On the other hand, it does inform us that apart from submission to God one will not attain an integrated and wholesome philosophy of life. It is noteworthy that the text promises that those whose search for truth begins with God will have "nourishment" in their "bones" (v. 8).

We do not encourage young people in the faith by scolding them for asking hard questions or by giving facile answers. Instead, we should seek to instill reverence for the mysterious wisdom of God, faith in the Bible, and belief that God's truth will stand the test of deep investigation.

Verses 9, 10 encourage us to give our material wealth to the work of God, and it adds the promise that He will repay us in full. This text could easily be distorted into a facile guarantee that God will enrich anyone who gives to the church. This passage is an encouragement to give that is based on the goodness of God, who looks upon the heart. It is not a supernatural get-rich-quick scheme.

Verses 11, 12, which are cited in Hebrews 12:5, 6, encourage us to submit to God's discipline. Unfortunately, most people think of "discipline" as "punishment," although much "discipline" is not punishment at all. In military training, recruits undergo harsh discipline that often involves no retribution for offenses; it is simply a matter of preparing the soldier for the rigors of combat.

One should accept all adversity as "discipline" from the hand of God meant for our training in righteousness, but one should not automatically assume that adversity equals punishment.

Verses 13–18 personify wisdom again as a woman. In a manner reminiscent of texts describing the acquisition of a good wife (Prov. 18:22), this text declares that the man who has obtained wisdom has gained something far more important than material wealth. Verses 13, 14 make the point that wisdom is well worth gaining, and verses 15–18 explain why she is so valuable. This text should put to rest the notion that Proverbs looks upon wisdom as the way to get rich; here, having wisdom contrasts with having wealth. Wisdom, unlike money, gives life and peace.

Verses 19, 20 continue to speak of the value of wisdom, but the focus shifts from wisdom as a life-giving woman to wisdom as an aspect of creation. This anticipates 8:22–31.

In verses 21–26, the second parental appeal, we read the primary reason for pursuing wisdom: It will preserve your life (v. 22). Using the metaphor of walking, it teaches us that wisdom helps us avoid the things that make us stumble. This can be anything from moral failure to poor social skills to careless handling of money. Wisdom helps us to live a life that is successful.

Verses 27–30 teach us how to be a neighbor to people. "Sins of omission" are the focus of verses 27, 28 (do not fail to do good to your neighbor) whereas "sins of commission" (do not plot to harm your neighbor) make up the focus of verses 29, 30.

Verses 31–35 flow naturally from verses 29, 30. This section continues the prohibitions against criminal behavior. Here, however, the focus is on the criminal, who is one of the two archetypal tempters that confront the young man (the other is the prostitute). The young man sees the power that the violent possess and is tempted to follow the path of getting what he wants through aggression, intimidation, and cruelty.

The Egyptians portrayed Maat, goddess of justice, as a woman holding the symbols of life and power. The Babylonian epic of Gilgamesh tells how the hero of the tale lost the plant of immortality. In the Bible, Adam and Eve lost access to the "tree of life" after their sin (Gen. 3:24). This text of Proverbs makes use of this ancient imagery to portray wisdom as a woman who holds life in her hands and is a tree of life.

But in God he confronts one stronger than himself; his destruction is certain.

- *In a general way, this text exhorts the reader*
- *to seek wisdom more than money or power.*
- *It focuses on the temptation to follow crime*
- *and cruelty and contrasts this with the life*
- *and peace that wisdom offers.*

FOURTH PARENTAL EXHORTATION (4:1–27)

This text is distinctive in that its focus is not so much on any particular moral issue as it is on the parental appeal itself. No one has a stronger desire to see a young man maintain a life of personal integrity and the fear of God than that young man's parents. Here, we see how intensely a father pleads with his son to do right and fear God. The opening parental appeal, which normally takes only a verse or two, here takes nine full verses. In the middle of this appeal the father identifies with his son's struggles by recalling how his own father taught him and appealed for him to do what is right.

The father knows from experience and from his own teachers that the message he is giving his son is right. He says he has "good precepts" (v. 2, NRSV) and he identifies his "commandments" (v. 4, NRSV) with "wisdom" (v. 5, NKJV). Using the now familiar personification of wisdom as a woman, he gives as his foundational advice: "Get wisdom!" (v. 5, NKJV).

In verses 10–19 the father returns to the image of the two ways. He emphasizes how those who follow wisdom do not "stumble" (v. 12) but move "along straight paths" (v. 11). He tells the

Parents must identify with their children as they teach them to do right. They can recall how they have faced similar moral decisions and how they also had elders trying to guide them in the right way. Young people must understand that they are not the first people to face moral challenges and hear advice from mother and father.

son not to "walk in the way of evil men" (v. 14). In addition, he asserts that the righteous walk in a way that gets brighter and clearer with the passing of time (v. 18) while the wicked stumble in darkness (v. 19).

In his close, the father continues to exhort his son in a general way to be faithful to wisdom (vv. 20–27). Here, the text makes use of metaphors that relate to the body. The eyes should hold to right teaching (vv. 21, 25) and the feet should stay in the right way (vv. 26, 27). The heart must be protected by the truth (vv. 21, 23). The mouth and lips should avoid perverse words (v. 24).

■ *This text is not notable for being original or*
■ *different; it repeats many ideas found in*
■ *other texts of Proverbs. It does, however,*
■ *portray the parental appeal as an act of deep*
■ *love. The father above all else wants the son*
■ *to do what is right. He makes no pretense of*
■ *giving original ideas; he repeats the old*
■ *truths he has heard from his father. They are*
■ *truths that stand the test of time.*

FIFTH PARENTAL EXHORTATION (5:1–23)

This text concerns sexual life. It warns against extramarital sexual relations and encourages the young man to wait and enjoy marital sexuality. As already described, the opening discourses of Proverbs focus heavily upon the two great temptations that confront the young man: the criminal, with the promise of easy money, and the prostitute, with the promise of easy sex.

In ancient Palestine, one type of prostitution was the sacred prostitution of the fertility cults. These were shrines dedicated to the Canaanite god Baal and the goddess Anat (also called Ashtarte). Sexual liaisons at the shrines between the prostitutes and their clients were supposed to provoke the gods to provide for fertility in the crops and livestock.

In verses 1–6, the opening section of chapter 5, the text warns against being attracted to the honeyed lips of the immoral woman because ultimately she gives only bitterness and death. It is important to observe that the book does not try to hide the fact that the woman is alluring. One cannot help young people avoid the temptation to sexual immorality without acknowledging that the appeal to sexual misconduct can be very strong, and not all of the appeal is physical. The smooth speech of the woman (v. 3) indicates that her personality is attractive. By admitting the reality of the temptation, the parent is better able to tell the youth why it is to be avoided.

The translation of verse 6 is difficult. As rendered in many versions (e.g., the NIV), it implies that the immoral woman is a lost soul who does not know that she is on the path to destruction. While this is no doubt true, in this text the woman is never an object of pity. She is a temptress who is leading other people to the grave. It is better understood to mean that she behaves as she does "so that you will fail to pay attention to the path of life. Her paths wander (from the way of life), but you will be unaware of it." In other words, verse 6 asserts that she leads the young man astray with her; it does not simply assert that she is lost.

In verses 15–19, the text exhorts the young man to derive all his sexual pleasure from his wife. The language of verse 19 is surprisingly straightforward; it encourages us to understand that sexuality is itself not the problem. Sexual pleasure between husband and wife is a gift from God. The wife and husband should exclusively "refresh" one another. Although not explicit, this text implicitly affirms monogamy over against polygamy.

The metaphors of verses 15, 16 are more difficult, but it appears that the "cistern" and "well" of verse 15 are the sexual affections of the wife and the "springs" and "streams of water" are the sexual affections of the husband.

Verses 20–23 conclude with the warning that those a who commit adultery fall under God's judgment. The penalty for such sin is more than guilty conscience or a public disgrace; it is also divine punishment.

- *This is the central text in Proverbs on the*
- *subject of sexual immorality. But the passage*
- *is not merely one of warning and censure. It*
- *offers a better way in the wholesome sexual*
- *life of monogamy.*

QUESTIONS TO GUIDE YOUR STUDY

1. What is it about gangs that appeals to some young men?
2. What is the value of wisdom in human life?
3. How do discipline and punishment differ?
4. What are the two ways of life set forth in Proverbs?
5. What are some consequences of sex outside God's guidelines?

PROVERBS 6–9 - - - -

THE FOUR TEACHINGS (6:1–19)

This chapter contains four distinct passages on different areas of wise behavior. The first, 6:1–5, concerns financial entanglements. The second, 6:6–11, concerns sloth versus diligence. The third, 6:12–15, concerns the behavior of the conspirator. The fourth, 6:16–19, gives a list of seven kinds of deadly sins.

The first teaching, verses 1–5, surprises readers because it seems to oppose generosity. This is not actually correct; it says nothing against giving money outright to another person. It warns us against getting into legal entanglements whereby our personal assets are in effect in the hands of another person, a person whose indebtedness does not recommend his good judgment. To cosign a note is often unwise because one no longer has control over one's financial future.

In verses 6–11, the text contrasts the laziness of the sluggard with the diligence of ants, the point being that even these tiny creatures have more sense than some humans. Verse 11 might be better translated, "And poverty will come upon you like a vagabond, and want will come like a beggar." Evidence for the traditional interpretation, "Like an armed warrior" (NRSV), is quite flimsy. The meaning is not that poverty will come upon the lazy man dramatically and unexpectedly. Rather, poverty and want will follow a lazy person like a persistent beggar who lingers outside one's home and always wants more.

In 6:12–15 we have a portrait of the conspirator as he uses signals to communicate with someone who is working with him in his scheme. Some people take the winking, shuffling, and pointing to be magical rituals, and others regard them as bawdy expressions of flirtation. But context supports neither view. The text describes this person as a scoundrel who sows discord and devises evil. It is best to take this as a description of general criminal or malicious behavior.

Christians have a traditional list of "seven deadly sins" (pride, anger, envy, impurity, gluttony, slothfulness, and avarice). In 6:16–19, we have an analogous list of seven things that the Lord

It is very difficult to lead a happy, peaceful life if one does not take steps to ensure a degree of financial well-being. This does not mean one trusts money rather than God. Christians get into financial trouble not because of too much faith in God but because of too little prudence in handling money. Financial problems can cause enormous distress and do severe damage to family life.

hates. It appears that the list was meant to be easily memorized. The first five items move generally from the top of the body (the eyes) to the bottom (the feet). In addition, this text has the form of a numerical saying ("six things . . . seven"), which is probably further indication that it was meant to be memorized.

"Haughty eyes" imply an arrogant spirit that will not submit to God. A "lying tongue" represents a person who has no regard for truth. Such a person has set himself above standards of right and wrong and is probably psychologically unhealthy. "Hands that shed innocent blood" refers to the violent personality. A "heart that devises wicked schemes" is a person who has no regard for anything except what may benefit him. "Feet that are quick to rush into evil" describes a person who is enthusiastic about the opportunity to do wrong. The "false witness" and the "man who stirs up dissension" seek to undermine justice and cooperation in society.

■ *In four teachings, this chapter gives us basic*
■ *rules for living. Fiscal prudence, diligence in*
■ *work, avoidance of malicious people, and*
■ *remembering basic teachings about sins to*
■ *avoid—all of these contribute to a whole-*
■ *some life.*

SIXTH PARENTAL EXHORTATION (6:20–35)

Parents naturally have concerns over whether their children will be able to resist the fire of libido and remain chaste until marriage. They know that sexual immorality carries with it many severe problems. These include the warping of one's moral character, dangers from sexually transmitted diseases, and the likelihood that bad decisions in this area of life will lead to bad decisions in many other areas of life.

In this text, both mother and father appeal to the young man to avoid sexual misbehavior (v. 20). The opening exhortation to bind the parents' commands about the neck (vv. 21–23) are very general in nature and could apply to any number of areas of life, but the rest of the text makes it clear that promiscuity is the real concern of this passage.

The specific danger that this text points out is that if one commits adultery, the outraged husband of the woman will come and exact his revenge upon the young man. One might flippantly respond, of course, that no such danger exists if the woman is not married. The point, however, is that there are many dangers associated with immorality; this text focuses only on one. Verse 26 is difficult to translate, but a fairly literal reading is: "Although the price of a prostitute may be (only) as much as a loaf of bread, another man's wife (actually) hunts his precious life."

The idea is that a prostitute might only charge a small amount for her services, but the ultimate price one pays for dalliance with her is very high indeed: It will cost you your life. The injured husband will ruin you, if not kill you outright.

■ *Parents must watch as the little children they*
■ *have brought into the world go out and make*
■ *decisions of their own. Nevertheless, they do*
■ *not send children out unarmed. By teaching*
■ *them right from wrong in the area of sexual*
■ *immorality (and by providing a good exam-*
■ *ple), parents can prepare children to meet*
■ *this powerful temptation.*

SEVENTH PARENTAL EXHORTATION (7:1–27)

This is another plea from the father that his son avoid the immoral woman. It is distinctive for having a lengthy story (vv. 6–23), bracketed by two appeals from the father (vv. 1–5, 24–27). In the example story, the father tells of a young man who senselessly followed the siren call of the immoral woman as it led him to the grave.

This text in particular shows us how important it is to consider the original context and audience of a text when making judgments about the meaning and value of that text. Many readers are offended at the fact that this text seems to portray the young man as the innocent victim while the woman is a wicked temptress and a guide to corruption. For this reason, some argue that the Bible represents a "sexist" view of the world; it is an outlook, they say, that presents women as fundamentally corrupt and dangerous. This supposedly fits in with a patriarchal viewpoint that dominates the Bible. After all, someone might say, are there not many (if not more) examples of gullible young women whose lives have been ruined by lusty, smooth-talking young men?

In fact, this interpretation completely misses the point of this passage. The text warns against immoral women not because women are morally inferior to men but because the implied reader of this text is the young man. It hardly makes sense to have a text that warns girls to stay away from seductive boys if the readers are young men.

Furthermore, the culture of ancient Israel was quite different from the modern West in an important respect. Today, the young men and women freely mingle on a social level, and there are many opportunities for boys who are looking for sex to seek the favor of their female peers in school and on the job. Thus, a chapter of warnings directed at young girls would make sense in this context. In ancient Israel, in which girls from "nice" families would have been more sequestered and have little unsupervised contacts with boys, the only girls to whom a young man was likely to go for sex was the prostitute or adulteress, a woman who would be more likely the seducer than the seduced. As such, in this context, with this intended audience, Proverbs 7 makes perfect sense and need not be regarded as a case of sexist oppression from a religious establishment.

In studying the Bible, beware of any interpretation that attributes wrong motives to the authors. These interpretations often arise from a failure to take seriously the original context of a text.

Perhaps the strangest thing about this seduction is that the woman speaks of her religious duties in verse 14. Some interpreters think that she means that she has just sacrificed an animal and is here offering the man a sumptuous meal. But the text says nothing else about a feast; throughout the passage she makes it very clear that she is taking him home for sex. Also, a better translation for verse 14 is not past tense but, "Peace offerings are due from me; today I am fulfilling my vows."

So understood, the passage means that she needs money to pay her religious vows and is using this as an excuse for her prostitution. Note that she also claims that her husband has taken a trip with the money and thus she will be without funds for a long time. In a weird kind of way, her words would assuage the young man's conscience. Paying for her services cannot be all bad if it helps to pay for a religious vow! The whole story is a fabrication, however; verse 13 says she speaks to him "with a brazen face." In other words, it is a straight-faced lie. The young dupe walks through her door, unaware that he is walking into a tomb.

- Using an example story, the father pleads
- with his son not to give into charm, lies, and
- available sex that the prostitute offers. He
- does not hide the fact that she has many plea-
- sures to offer (vv. 16–18), but he warns that
- the price for her pleasures is far too high; it
- is the young man's life.

SECOND WISDOM APPEAL (8:1–36)

Lady Wisdom made her first appeal in 1:20–33. The most significant question confronting the reader is, Who is Lady Wisdom? Some say she is a mythological figure or an Israelite goddess. This is certainly incorrect. Even Egyptian wisdom literature did not regard wisdom as a goddess; it is unthinkable that Israelite literature would. Evangelical readers are more likely to think that wisdom is Christ on the basis of 1 Corinthians 1:24, which calls Christ "the wisdom of God." This would be, however, a misreading both of Proverbs 8 and of Paul.

When Paul speaks of Christ as the "wisdom of God," he means that the historical Person and event, the crucified Jesus Christ, is God's profound means of bringing salvation to humanity. What Greeks regarded as absolute foolishness—that a crucified Jew should be God's appointed Savior of the world—was in fact profound truth. But this does not mean that any text on wisdom is really a text about Jesus Christ. By analogy, John tells us that "God is love" (1 John 4:8), but this does not mean that

1 Corinthians 13 is a text that is, strictly speaking, about God.

Lady Wisdom of Proverbs 8 is not a goddess, or God, or even an attribute of God. She is an attribute of creation. She is a personification of the wisdom that God has built into the world. When she describes her role in creation (8:22–31), her point is that because principles of wisdom are woven into the creation fabric, no one can survive long if he violates the teachings of wisdom. The world and the human soul are made in such a way that those who are prudent, diligent, trustworthy, and chaste as a general rule will be emotionally, physically, and even financially healthy.

By contrast, those who are treacherous, reckless, and immoral destroy themselves. Those who follow the way of folly live a life that contradicts the structure of the world. They are like people who use pure nitroglycerin as fuel in an ordinary car and think that it will do no damage to the engine.

In verses 1–3, Lady Wisdom is not in the academy or in the cloistered world of a sacred priesthood, but in the streets and markets calling for people to come to her. She is not for an elite few but for ordinary people. In verses 4–11, she says that her words are right and forthright. There is no craftiness or treachery in her teachings. They are plain and true. Verses 13–16 assert that wisdom gives one a hatred for evil but also gives one the ability to lead. Verses 17–21 tell us that wisdom leads us to prosperity not by magic or by underhanded means, but by teaching us that if we play by the rules of life, things will generally go well for us. Verses 22–31 focus on wisdom's place in creation. She is the pattern by

Sexual immorality is wrong not just because God forbids it but because we are made for heterosexual monogamy. Sexually transmitted diseases are an example of how creation itself does not allow for promiscuity. The psychology of the human soul also suffers great damage when people are immoral.

25

which the world is made. Verses 32–36 close with a restatement of the doctrine of the two ways: Those who follow her will find life; those who do not will die.

■ *Wisdom is built into creation itself. With it,*
■ *one can live a good and wholesome life.*
■ *Without it, one is shipwrecked against the*
■ *rocks of rules that were ignored too long.*

THE TWO INVITATIONS (9:1–18)

This text draws together all the exhortations of chapters 1–8 and presents the reader with a simple choice about the two ways. The way of wisdom is espoused by Lady Wisdom in verses 1–12 and the way of folly is proclaimed by a new character, Woman Folly, in verses 13–18. Woman Folly is obviously the counterpart to Lady Wisdom, but she also has the characteristics of the prostitute. She is loud and careless and is a temptress (see 7:11).

The appeal of Lady Wisdom is in three parts: first, the appeal to come to her banquet (vv. 1–6); second, a description of a "mocker" (vv. 7–9); and third, her summation of the meaning of true wisdom (vv. 10–12). It is not clear why her house has seven pillars (archaeologists have found shrines with seven pillars, but it is not certain that the existence of these shrines has any relevance for this text). Probably the number seven represents the seven days of Creation; chapter 8 ties the understanding of wisdom to the Creation account. Also, we cannot be sure why she sends out her servants, but it may be that they are to invite her guests. The text reminds one of the parable of the great banquet in Luke 14:15–24.

Jesus warned His disciples not to cast pearls before pigs (Matt. 7:6). The appeal of Lady Wisdom, similarly, recognizes that some people are "mockers" who will not just reject but scorn and pervert wisdom. In a truism that is almost ironic, the text tells us that wisdom is for the wise in verses 7–9.

Verses 10, 11 describe three foundational teachings of wisdom. First, true wisdom begins with piety (v. 10). Second, wisdom gives long life and prosperity (v. 11). Third, the wages of wisdom and folly are as dramatically different as life and death.

The account of Woman Folly obviously parodies Lady Wisdom. She, too, is in her house and she, too, invites her guests to a meal (of bread and water!). It may be that verse 17 looks back to the two temptations (the prostitute for easy sex and the criminal associate for easy money). "Stolen water" looks back to 5:15–18, where sexual relations are described as the drinking of water. "Food eaten in secret" (literally, the "bread of secrecy") looks back to the criminal groups described in 1:11–14; 4:14–17; and 6:12–15.

■ *This chapter concludes the exhortations with*
■ *a clear statement of the two ways (here*
■ *described as two houses) that lie open before*
■ *the young man. He can either follow wisdom*
■ *to life and peace or folly to the grave.*

QUESTIONS TO GUIDE YOUR STUDY

1. What are some negative consequences of cosigning a note?
2. List seven things the Lord hates?
3. What does Lady Wisdom symbolize?

PROVERBS 10–14

- - - -

SUBTITLE (10:1a)

This verse is a subheading that separates the lengthy discourses of chapters 1–9 from the short proverbs that dominate the chapters that follow.

A DILIGENT SON AND A LAZY SON (10:1b–5)

This set of five proverbs is bracketed by the proverb of verse 1 with that of verse 5, both of which contrast the wise son with the foolish or disgraceful son. It is fitting that such a group of proverbs should immediately follow chapters 1–9, chapters that are dominated by parental appeals to the son. The three proverbs in verses 2–4 concern the matter of acquiring wealth. Three distinct ideas are present.

Parents who neglect the training of their children do themselves economic damage. They have to bail out grown children who should be taking care of themselves if not helping the parents as well.

First, one should acquire money only by lawful and moral means (v. 2); the verse implies that those who acquire wealth by unlawful means will be brought down to the grave. Second, one should depend on the Lord for food, shelter, and clothing (v. 3). Third, one should work hard if one expects to prosper (v. 4). Verse 5 links the idea of the wise and the foolish son to biblical teachings on prosperity. A family's well being depends in great measure on whether sons grow to become responsible or become freeloaders.

THE MOUTH OF THE WICKED (10:6–11)

Verses 6–11 are a simple presentation of how the wicked differ from the righteous, with some emphasis on the "mouth" of the wicked (i.e., their lies, perjury, and acts of fraud). Throughout the passage, there is a heavy emphasis on how the wicked use dissimulation to cover their crimes. Verses 6 and 11 bracket the text in that both have the line, "The mouth of the wicked conceals violence" (NRSV). Within those two bracketing verses, verses 7–10 have a parallel pattern. That is, verse 7 parallels verse 9 in that both talk about how the destiny of the wicked contrasts with the righteous. Verse 8 parallels verse 10 in that both have the line, "A babbling fool will come to ruin" (NRSV). The malicious wink of verse 10 is probably a sign among conspirators and is another example of the deceitful tactics of the wicked.

SEVEN-PROVERB COLLECTION (10:12–18)

This is another series of proverbs with an inclusion or bracket structure. Verse 12 contrasts a forgiving spirit with an implacable spirit. Verse 18 should be translated in accordance with the rendition in the Septuagint as, "He who forgives hatred has righteous lips, but he who spreads defamation is a fool." Thus, like verse 12, it contrasts forgiveness with verbal retaliation.

The Septuagint is the ancient Greek translation of the Hebrew Old Testament. It is sometimes helpful in understanding difficult Hebrew passages. It is commonly abbreviated LXX.

By itself, verse 13 makes little sense because it is hard to see how the second half of the verse relates to the first. Verse 14, however, makes the thought complete: The wise store knowledge and give intelligent answers, but fools blurt out offensive or absurd words and receive a beating.

Verse 15, by itself, seems to say little more than that one is better off rich than poor. Verse 16,

Verse 17 teaches that one must accept discipline in his or her life before trying to lead others. The leader who has never learned to submit and accept correction destroys his followers. A pastor who cannot bear to be corrected will not be able to correct others.

which also uses the economic terms *wages* and *riches*, provides moral balance: Money wrongfully gained drags a person to the grave. Together, these verses make the point that it is better to have money than to be without, but that money wrongfully gained destroys a person. Verse 17 looks back to verses 13 and 14 with the contrast between words of the wise, which lead to life, and the words of the wicked, which lead people astray.

ON THE TONGUE, PERSONAL SECURITY, AND LAZINESS (10:19–32)

This section is a collection of five texts arranged in chiastic fashion, as follows:

A: The use of the mouth (vv. 19–21)
    B: Personal security (vv. 22–25)
        C: Laziness (v. 26)
    B′: Personal security (vv. 27–30)
A′: The use of the mouth (vv. 31, 32)

Both verses 19–21 and verses 31, 32 focus on the "tongue," "words," "mouth," and "lips." Similarly, verses 22–25 and verses 27–30 deal with issues of longevity, prosperity, and the ability to withstand calamities, and both are four-verse collections. Also, verse 22 begins with "the blessing of the LORD" and verse 27 with "the fear of the LORD." It is curious that a proverb on laziness stands at the center; this perhaps reflects the fact that people who are lazy tend toward foolish use of the tongue and toward personal ruin.

THE USE OF THE MOUTH (10:19–21)

Verses 20 and 21 are closely linked. Together they assert that the wise teach and strengthen others with their words but fools are senseless and suffer the consequences. The two metaphors for the words of the wise are different but complementary. They are "like silver" in that they are of high value; they "feed many" in the sense that they give life and strength. Verse 19 introduces this pair with a saying on how one can tell the wise from the foolish (and thus know to whom one should listen): The foolish are verbose!

PERSONAL SECURITY (10:22–25)

These proverbs have a series of lessons on wealth and security. These include, first, the righteous have their wishes fulfilled without having the bitter experience of discovering that the things they desired have given them more pain than pleasure (vv. 22, 24). Second, the wicked enjoy doing evil but have no ability to withstand troubles (vv. 23, 25). Third, the troubles that the wicked fear will in fact come upon them (v. 24), but the righteous will endure hard times and ultimately have a life characterized by well being (v. 25).

SINGLE PROVERB (10:26)

Smoke is irritating and vinegar is bitter. Lazy people are irritating because they never do their assigned tasks and make others bitter. They always want others to meet their needs.

PERSONAL SECURITY (10:27–30)

These verses essentially repeat the sentiments of verses 22–25. It is important to recognize that the primary source of security for the wise is not their wisdom but the faithfulness of God. Proverbs speaks a great deal about integrity, common sense, and diligence, but it never implies that these are enough. Even the most decent and sensible people are lost without the grace of God.

THE USE OF THE MOUTH (10:31, 32)

These two proverbs go together to teach that the righteous give sound advice and can speak appropriately in any situation. The wicked, however, twist the truth to their own advantage and lead others astray with their warped value system. The statement that the wicked will have their tongues "cut out" is probably a metaphor. It means that no one will listen to them any more so that they are effectively silenced.

MORAL INTEGRITY AND GOD'S JUDGMENT (11:1–4)

These four verses are arranged in chiastic fashion, as follows:

A: God's hatred of fraud (v. 1)
   B: Pride versus humility (v. 2)
   B´: Integrity versus crookedness (v. 3)
A´: Wealth useless on the day of judgment (v. 4)

Some Christians may be troubled by passages like this and suppose that Proverbs endorses "works righteousness." Such fear would be misguided; Proverbs never asserts that one attains forgiveness by appeasing God with good works. On the other hand, this fear indicates that many Christians do not really understand justification by grace. God's grace does not mean that one need not repent or that God is indifferent to how we conduct our lives. A person who is content to live a selfish, devious life has not truly repented.

There is an obvious link between verse 1 and verse 4; the first teaches that God hates fraudulent business practices and verse 4 states that wealth (by implication that was wrongfully gained) does a person no good when facing an angry God. Individually, verses 2 and 3 are so simple and straightforward as to be little more than truisms. Together, they imply that pride leads to a treacherous mentality and that humility is a prerequisite for true wisdom.

SALVATION FOR THE RIGHTEOUS (11:5, 6)

These two verses make the simple claim that the righteous thrive in their righteousness, and the evil are destroyed by their sins.

DEATH OF A SINNER (11:7, 8)

These two verses contrast the fate of the wicked with that of the righteous. When the wicked die, whatever hopes they had die with them. This implies a contrast with the righteous; and if the hope of the righteous does not die with them, then by implication they inherit some kind of afterlife or resurrection. Verse 8, by contrast, deals with this world. In an almost ironic tone, it suggests that life really is unfair: God heaps troubles on the wicked and saves the righteous from their mistakes!

DESTRUCTIVE LIPS (11:9–13)

Verses 9–12 are chiastic in structure. Verses 9 and 12 describe how the wicked belittle and destroy people with their words, and verses 10 and 11 speak of how the righteous and the wicked affect the well being of their city. Taken together, the four proverbs imply that those who provoke conflicts with their gossip and verbal attacks bring down the quality of life in any community. Verse 13 confirms this with an extra saying on gossip.

NATIONAL AND PERSONAL PRUDENCE (11:14, 15)

Verse 15 is an oft-repeated proverb warning against cosigning loans (see 6:1; 17:18; 20:16; 22:26; 27:13). Verse 14, however, concerns prudence in national affairs. Perhaps these two have been juxtaposed to remind us that we must be wise in dealing with all affairs, whether they are large or small.

KINDNESS AND CRUELTY (11.16–21)

These verses contrast the outcome of decent behavior with the outcome of ruthlessness. By itself, verse 16 could be taken as a cynical statement (the word "only" in the NIV is not in the Hebrew), if one wanted to claim that wealth is better than respect. Verse 17, however, adds the corrective thought that even if ruthless people do get rich, they destroy themselves in the

We are often driven to despair by the violence and injustice in society. We must remember that although human justice fails, God's justice never does.

process. Verses 18, 19 add in a fairly straightforward manner that people will get what they deserve. Still, the reader may be unsure that this is true, and verses 20, 21 gives the assurance that God Himself is determined to maintain moral order in the world and that he will give people the punishment they deserve.

BEAUTY WITHOUT DISCRETION (11:22)

The point of this proverb is that beauty has been given to someone who does not deserve it.

GENEROSITY AND SELFISHNESS (11:23–27)

Everyone knows that people despise selfish, greedy people and love those who are generous. This passage goes beyond matters of popularity to observe the paradox that generous people always seem to have enough and hoarders lose the possessions they love. This paradox is not an accident; it is part of the wisdom that God has built into the world.

THE SOURCE OF LIFE (11:28–12:4)

Proverbs 11:28, 29 are paralleled by 12:3, 4. Proverbs 11:28 and 12:3 use the metaphor of the tree to contrast the security of the righteous with the demise of the wicked. Proverbs 11:29 and 12:4 teach how important a man's family life is to his well-being. Proverbs 11:30 is often taken as a verse on evangelism. The three verses that follow (11:31–12:2) contrast the way of the righteous with the way of the evil, which further indicates that this is how 11:30 should be taken.

The Hebrew phrase translated "wins souls," however, actually means to "kill." The verse should probably be rendered, "The fruit of the righteous is a tree of life, but violence takes away lives."

PLANS AND SCHEMES (12:5–7)

These proverbs have a logical progression. The righteous make just plans, but the wicked scheme (v. 5). The wicked ambush the righteous, but the righteous are delivered by integrity (v. 6). The wicked are destroyed, and the righteous stand secure (v. 8).

EARNED RESPECT (12:8)
People are praised for their integrity and their ability to solve problems, two aspects of wisdom.

ON PROVIDING FOR NEEDS (12:9–11)
All of these proverbs in some fashion concern providing for needs. Prosperity is better than feigned status (v. 9), and prosperity only comes by hard work and not by chasing delusive dreams (v. 11). The righteous provide even for their animals; the wicked only exploit (v. 10).

Dreams of winning the lottery would be a modern example of this.

ON FRUIT AND SNARES (12:12, 13)
The beginning of verse 12 should be translated, "The wicked takes pleasure in a net of evil men." It means that they appreciate those who trap and rob people. Verse 13, however, says that the wicked will themselves be trapped.

FRUIT FROM ONE'S LIFE (12:14)
The righteous gain benefit from what they say as well as how hard they work.

ABLE TO TAKE ADVICE (12:15)
The meaning of this text is fairly clear: People who think they do not need advice are the real fools.

THE USE AND ABUSE OF WORDS (12:16–22)
Almost every proverb in this series relates to the use of words, whether it be for good or ill. Verbal quarrels (v. 16), honesty (vv. 17, 19, 23), and tact (v. 18) are the major issues here. The exceptions are verses 20 and 21, although verse 20 does speak of deceit "in the hearts" of the wicked, so presumably it is on their lips also. In this context, moreover, the righteous and wicked who receive rewards and punishments,

respectively (v. 21), are probably those who use their words for either good or for evil.

A WHOLESOME LIFE (12:23–28)

These six proverbs have a parallel pattern, as follows:

A: Caution and imprudence (v. 23)
   B: Diligence and laziness (v. 24)
      C: Anxiety and joy (v. 25)
A´: Caution and imprudence (v. 26)
   B´: Diligence and laziness (v. 27)
      C´: Life and death (v. 28)

These verses do not follow a single theme but describe things that make for a wholesome life (prudence, diligence, and joy) or an early death (lack of caution, laziness, or anxiety). Contrary to the NIV, verse 28 does not deal with immortality. The end of verse 28 should simply be rendered, "Along that way there is no death" (that is, it is a safe path to take).

THE USE OF THE MOUTH (13:1–4)

Every proverb in this passage relates somehow to the mouth. The wise son gives heed to what comes out of his father's mouth, but the mocker does not (v. 1). Verses 2 and 4 assert that the upright "eat" good things (that is, they enjoy the benefits of their way of life), whereas the wicked "crave" violence and are always hungry but not satisfied (that is, they are driven by their appetites but never find fulfillment). Verse 3 warns the reader to guard the words of his mouth.

RIGHTEOUSNESS AND WICKEDNESS (13:5, 6)

Verse 5 should be translated, "A righteous man hates a lie, but a wicked man makes a stench and causes shame." The point appears to be that the righteous care about the truth and therefore hate gossip, whereas the evil foster scandal, often by telling lies. Verse 6 therefore means that the righteous are preserved from infamy but that it brings down the wicked.

THE AMBIGUITY OF RICHES (13:7–11)

Verses 7, 8, and 10 deal with financial prosperity. Verse 7 could be taken to mean simply that external appearances are not always a sure guide to how large a person's bank account is. On a more profound level, it may be that those who "pretend to be rich" are actually arrogant people who, no matter how much money they have, actually have nothing. Those who live as though they are poor probably are not deceptive but simply humble and able to live modestly. This would tie in with the saying on quarrelsome arrogance in verse 10; those who pompously act wealthy would be the kind who readily get into conflicts.

Verse 8 warns the reader that having wealth is not all that it seems: the wealthy face troubles that never bother a person of modest means. Verse 9 tells us that true security, symbolized by a burning lamp, is in godliness. Verse 11 contrasts the ephemeral quality of money gained quickly but dishonestly with the secure wealth of money gradually and honestly accrued.

A HOPE FULFILLED (13:12–19)

Verses 12 and 19 speak of how people desire to have their longings fulfilled. Between these two, verses 13–18 speak of how important it is to listen to the instruction of the wise, to act with knowledge, and to accept correction.

We can realize the dreams of our hearts if we pay attention to wise instruction and live accordingly.

CHOICE COMPANIONS (13:20–21)

Verse 20 warns us to be careful about whom we choose as companions. Verse 21 should be read in the light of verse 20 because young people often fall in with bad companions precisely because they think they will help them get easy money (see Prov. 1:11–14). The point of verse 21 is that youth should not be enticed by evil companions who seem to have it all. They lead people to ruin, not to riches.

PROVISION FOR THE FAMILY (13:22–25)

These four proverbs make for an amazing bit of parallelism, as follows:

A: A good man leaves his children an inheritance; an evil man does not (v. 22).

    B: Poor people go hungry because of the injustice of the rich (v. 23).

A´: A good man disciplines his children; an evil man does not (v. 24).

    B´: Righteous people have food; the evil go hungry (v. 25).

This passage shows something of how complicated life is. The wise give their children a material inheritance (because they have not squandered their money), but they also give them a material inheritance (v. 24). Families often go hungry because the parents have been lazy or foolish with money (e.g., through gambling or substance abuse). On the other hand, sometimes people suffer want through no fault of their own but because of the evil of others (v. 23).

SELF-PROTECTIVE AND SELF-DESTRUCTIVE BEHAVIOR (14:1–3)

Verse 1 states that a wise woman builds her house while a foolish one destroys hers, and verse 3 states that a foolish man invites a beating with his words (be they insults or lies) while a wise man's lips do him good. Between these two, verse 2 states that the key to determining whether one's life will follow right or wrong is in whether that person fears God.

A WORTHWHILE INVESTMENT (14:4)

This should be translated, "In the absence of oxen there is a feed trough full of grain, but in the strength of the bull there is abundant harvest." A person must make an investment (buy an ox and extra grain to feed it) to get a return.

LOOK WHO'S TALKING (14:5–7)

These proverbs carry a simple lesson: Be careful about who you listen to.

APPEARANCE AND REALITY (14:8–15)

This text generally warns that appearances can be deceptive. It has a chiastic structure, as follows:

A: The prudent think about what lies ahead, but fools are easily deceived (v. 8).
  B: Fools refuse to make amends for sins (v. 9).
    C: Everyone has secrets (v. 10).
      D: The house of the wicked will be destroyed (v. 11).
      D´: The way that seems right leads to death (v. 12).
    C´: Everyone has hidden pain (v. 13).
  B´: The wicked are fully repaid for sins (v. 14).
A´: The prudent think about what lies ahead, but fools are easily deceived (v. 15).

If these verses have anything in common, it is that life is often not what it seems to be and that one must be discerning. Verses 8 and 15 distinguish the foresight of the wise from the gullibility of fools. Verse 9 indicates that some people think they can avoid making amends for their sins, but verse 14 says that this never really happens. Verses 10 and 12 distinguish the outward demeanor of a person from the true state of the heart. A house seems more permanent than a tent, but verse 11 observes that the house of the wicked will fall where the tent of the righteous

True security is in God and an upright life. If a person has these, even life in a tent can be stable and secure. Without them, there is no security, no matter how great one's house is.

The Bible demands that we work hard (14:23) and show compassion to the poor (14:21). To do one without the other is to have a partial morality.

will endure. Similarly, a person may think that his "way" is right when in reality it leads to death.

A PATIENT SPIRIT (14:16, 17)

These verses address the need for prudence before action. They should be translated, "A wise man is cautious and stays out of trouble, but a fool is hotheaded and reckless. A quick-tempered man does foolish things, but a thinking man endures provocation."

A CROWN OF WISDOM, A WREATH OF FOLLY (14:18–24)

Verse 18 and verse 24 describe the crown of the wise in contrast to the inheritance of folly; they thus bracket this text. Verse 19 adds that the evil will bow to the good. Verses 21, 22 generally contrast the scheming and cruelty of the evil with the benevolence of the righteous. Verse 20 speaks of the plight of the poor, while verse 23 asserts that a person must work hard to avoid poverty.

AN HONEST WITNESS (14:25)

The courts are apparently in view here, and the point is that perjury is a matter of life and death.

THE FEAR OF THE LORD (14:26, 27)

The fear of the Lord is a fortress in the sense that it gives security and a source of life in that it turns us from the moral pitfalls that destroy us.

A KING AND HIS FOLLOWERS (14:28–35)

Verse 28 asserts that a king needs followers, and verse 35 asserts that a king's subject needs the king's approval. Thus, there is a reciprocal relationship between the two. Verses 29–32 are more individual in nature and emphasize that the righteous thrive in all circumstances but that the evil fail. Verse 32, however, is probably best rendered, "When trouble comes, the wicked man is cast down, but a righteous man seeks refuge in integrity." Verse 33 also has a translation problem; it should probably be rendered, "Wisdom reposes in the heart of the discerning, but among fools she is unknown."

Verse 34 gives the general maxim that an evil nation is weak but a moral nation is strong.

■ *Proverbs 14:28–35 is something of a miscel-*
■ *laneous collection, but it is noteworthy that it*
■ *begins and ends by talking about the rela-*
■ *tionship of a ruler to his people. The inter-*
■ *vening proverbs speak of the differences*
■ *between righteous and evil individuals, and*
■ *verse 34 makes the summarizing statement*
■ *that only a righteous nation will thrive. The*
■ *overall point seems to be that the security of*
■ *a nation resides in the righteousness of indi-*
■ *vidual citizens.*

QUESTIONS TO GUIDE YOUR STUDY

1. How do the wise and fools differ in their use of speech?
2. What are some of the consequences of ill-gotten gain?
3. What warnings does Proverbs give to those who are hotheaded?

TWO COLLECTIONS (15:1–16:8)

This text is essentially a collection of miscellaneous proverbs, although it does seem to have two major sections (15:1–17 and 15:18–16:8). Proverbs 15:1 and 15:18 describe gentleness with a harsh and angry spirit, and 15:16, 17 and 16:8 contain "better sayings" (proverbs that say, "better is X than Y") on true prosperity. Both major sections deal with the same topics, although not in the same order.

Proverbs 15:1 reminds us that we can generally avert a confrontation and often get the result we want if we approach a person with patience. Proverbs 15:2 and 4 assert that words of the wise heal and instruct while the words of the perverse hurt and confuse. Proverbs 15:3, between these two, remind us that God is ever watchful over the behavior of people, and by implication over what they say. Proverbs 15:5 describes the "wise son" and at the same time indicates that wisdom is found in those who know how to take advice rather than just give it.

Proverbs 15:6 describes two households that are financially well off; the similarity, however, ends there. The righteous home has only joy from its possessions, while the wicked household has only trouble. Proverbs 15:7, like verses 2 and 4, contrasts the speech of the wise with that of fools. Proverbs 15:8, 9 tells us that superficial religion is no substitute for integrity. Proverbs 15:10, 11 carries this a step further: God sees all, and He is a stern judge.

Proverbs 15:12–15 are four verses set in parallel. Verses 12 and 14 contrast the scoffer, who

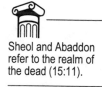

Sheol and Abaddon refer to the realm of the dead (15:11).

will not listen to instruction, with the wise, who will. Verses 13 and 15 contrast cheerfulness with sadness. By placing these two pairs of proverbs together in this fashion, the book implies that happiness comes by following sound teaching. Finally, 15:16, 17 asserts that contentment with the fear of God is better than riches.

Proverbs 15:18, like 15:1, implies that one should be calm in dealing with a potential adversary, and it implies that by this, one can avoid costly litigation. Just as 15:6 spoke of the household income of the righteous and the wicked, 15:19 describes the respective paths of these two types. The righteous, unlike sluggards, do not stumble from problem to problem. Proverbs 15:20, like 15:5, speaks of the wise and the foolish son. Whereas verse 5 only briefly speaks of listening to advice, 15:21, 22 gives more detailed instruction on decision making.

First, one should not veer off the basic path of wisdom (v. 21) and second, one should seek wise counsel in making decisions (v. 22). Proverbs 15:23 makes the observation that people enjoy it when they have just the right response to a question or argument. By implication, one should get wisdom in order to be able to do this.

Proverbs 15:24–27, like 15:3, focuses on divine retribution. People who do right thrive and those who do evil destroy themselves, both because right principles govern the world and because God himself enforces justice. Proverbs 15:28, like 15:7, contrasts the speech of the righteous with that of evil persons. It also gives a practical means for detecting the foolish or wicked speaker: he spews out whatever words come to mind.

"Fat on the bones" describes physical well-being (15:30, NASB).

Proverbs 15:29 implies that God rejects the prayers of the wicked just as 15:8 says he rejects their sacrifices. Proverbs 15:30 speaks of happiness and the health that comes from it.

Just as 15:13, 15 speaks of cheerfulness. Proverbs 15:31, 32 encourage us to listen to instruction and rebukes just as 15:12, 14 do. Together, these verse establish a strong link between happiness and the willingness to submit to sound instruction.

Proverbs 15:33–16:7 is unusual in proverbs; rarely does one see such a long passage that so explicitly speaks of the need to submit to the Lord (many proverbs speak abstractly of "wisdom" without explicitly mentioning the Lord). But this section has a parallel in 15:10, 11, which warns us that the Lord sees all and judges severely. Coming near the end of a lengthy text of instruction, 15:33–16:7 tells us that everything that matters (happiness, security, wisdom, patience, and so forth) comes from submission to God. Proverbs 16:8 closes this text with a better saying—that it is better to be righteous, though poor, than evil.

■ *In these two lengthy passages, similar teach-*
■ *ings on miscellaneous topics are repeated or*
■ *expanded. But this does not mean that there*
■ *is no plan to the passage. To the contrary, its*
■ *overall structure carries a very strong mes-*
■ *sage—all good things come from the fear of*
■ *God.*

THREE COLLECTIONS (16:9–17:1)

This is another lengthy collection of miscellaneous proverbs, but it appears to have an unusual structure of three parts, as follows:

A: Human plans and God's sovereignty (16:9)

　(Nine miscellaneous proverbs)

　B: "Better" sayings on humble circumstances (16:19)

A': Human plans and God's sovereignty (16:20)

　(Eleven miscellaneous proverbs)

　B': "Better" saying on patience (16:32)

A': Human plans and God's sovereignty (16:33)

　B': "Better" saying on humble circumstances (17:1)

Proverbs 16:9, 20, and 33 asserts that we can make our plans and concoct all kinds of devices for making decisions, but, ultimately, all things are in God's hands. Proverbs 16:19, 32, and 17.1 assert that the way that seems weaker—humility, patience, and scarcity—are better than their aggressive opposites. Proverbs 15:10–15 deals with government. One should not read these proverbs as an unequivocal assertion that the king is always right and righteous. They are teachings on how kings *ought* to behave, not how they actually do behave. Proverbs 16:16, 17 is a simple exhortation to get wisdom rather than riches, and 16:18 is the most famous maxim in Proverbs on pride. It is probably not accidental that these verses follow a portrait of an ideal monarch. Such a king should seek understanding more than riches, and above all he should fear the trap of pride.

One is reminded of the Beatitudes, (Matt. 5:3–11).

Proverbs 16:21–25 expands the teaching on how important it is to gain wisdom. These words seem especially suited to those in positions of leadership and high responsibility. Proverbs 16:27–30 lists types of persons one should avoid, including conspirators, gossips, and belligerent people. These proverbs are valid for anyone, but again, they seem especially apt as applied to a ruler, who must carefully judge people and decide in whom to place confidence.

Proverbs 16:26 seems odd, asserting that the hunger of a laborer drives him on. This too, however, seems to be given for the benefit of a ruler, who must try to govern fairly but not indulgently. Verse 31 also appears to have special relevance for kings: They may wear crowns, but they can live long enough to have a "crown" of gray hair only by righteousness. This is a reminder that the king who governs foolishly is likely to be assassinated!

■ *The proverbs of 16:9–17:1 have wide appli-*
■ *cation and can be used by anyone, but they*
■ *seem to have special significance for kings.*
■ *For them, the task of gaining wisdom, main-*
■ *taining humility, discerning the moral char-*
■ *acter of people, and learning to submit to the*
■ *sovereignty of God is particularly critical.*

PERSONS OF QUALITY (17:2, 3)

Verse 2 tells us that ability and quality can overcome the disadvantages of low birth. Verse 3 implies that the Lord tests people's character by adversity, symbolized by the heat of the crucible.

WARNINGS ABOUT MALICE (17:4, 5)

Verse 4 warns us that if we pay heed to malicious gossip, we are ourselves wicked. Verse 5, similarly, warns us that we make fun of God if we make fun of suffering people.

TRUE TREASURE (17:6)

A crown represents two things most people seek: power and wealth. The point here is that family is the real treasure one should seek to preserve.

> If parents do not make the raising of children a priority and if children (of any age) do not honor their parents, both risk losing the greatest joy that life can offer.

EXERCISING LEADERSHIP (17:7, 8)

By itself, verse 8 simply states that a bribe works—an idea that could be read very cynically. After verse 7, however, the implication is that the focus of the text is on good leadership. A real leader does not govern through deceit (v. 7) or take advantage of his power to get rich through bribery.

THE SOCIAL AND ANTISOCIAL (17:9–13)

This is a chiasmus, as follows:

A: Gracious forgiveness (v. 9)
   B: Irrationality of a fool (v. 10)
      C: Punishment for a rebel (v. 11)
   B′: Irrationality of a fool (v. 12)
A′: Irrational retaliation (v. 13)

Those who can forgive an offense will maintain good friendships, whereas those who broadcast the misdeeds of others will find themselves friendless (v. 9). But the attitude of forgiveness in verse 10a especially contrasts with the irrational behavior of those who harm others that have been kind to them (v. 13). Verse 10 tells us that the fool is stubbornly wrongheaded, no matter how much it hurts. This agrees with verse 12, which tells us that fools are dangerous to be near.

Together, these verses tell us that they are obstinate and destructive. This naturally leads to the middle proverb, verse 11, that describes the punishment that comes upon rebels. The "cruel messenger" may be a magistrate charged with punishing those who disturb the order of society.

■ *Together, these verses present a picture of*
■ *social and antisocial behavior. The former is*
■ *characterized by an ability to forgive and to*
■ *receive correction—a gentle spirit. The lat-*
■ *ter is gossipy, retaliatory, headstrong, and*
■ *destructive of order in society. Such people*
■ *are "rebels" in that they cannot handle*
■ *authority.*

QUICK TO QUARREL (17:14–19)

Like 17:9 and 13, verses 14 and 19 deal with the issue of quarrels. Verse 14 advises the reader to avoid them if at all possible, and verse 19 says that those who are evil and hostile bring many quarrels down on their own heads. It is not likely, however, that these are simple shouting matches; the "quarrels" here are probably disagreements that evolve into expensive lawsuits. Verse 15, therefore, although it makes sense by itself, perhaps speaks against those who promote injustice and strife by siding with the guilty party in a legal dispute.

Verses 16–18 focus on money. It may be that these verses appear here because money is so often at the heart of legal disputes. Verse 16 tells us that fools cannot handle money, and verse 18 repeats the frequent maxim that one should not cosign a loan. Both of these proverbs make good sense by themselves, but in this context the implied point may be that the fool's mishandling of money—especially when it comes to handling debt—invites legal quarrels. Nevertheless, Proverbs does not allow us to turn this into a pretext for selfishness. Verse 17 reminds us that those who know how to love will help their friends in time of trouble.

HEART AND FAMILY (17:20–22)

Each of these proverbs makes sense by itself, but there is a kind of progression. A man with a twisted heart and mind (as reflected in his words) falls into all kinds of trouble (v. 20). The father of such a man is full of sorrow (v. 21). The sadness in his family life gives the father such deep depression that it threatens his health (v. 22). These verses tell us that how our children live will either lift our spirits or bring us down to the grave in sadness.

The deeper message of this text is that we cannot find happiness if we neglect to train, love, and nurture our children. No amount of success in other areas will make up for failure here.

JUSTICE AND FAMILY (17:23–26)

Verses 23 and 26 describe the miscarriages of justice that result when people accept bribes from litigants. The wrong is victorious and the upright are fined or beaten. This context may explain the enigmatic verse 24, which says, "Wisdom is in the presence of the one who has understanding, But the eyes of a fool are on the ends of the earth" (NASB). The discerning have a moral gravity about them that refuses to be involved in corruption or the perversion of justice, but fools look off to the ends of the earth in the sense of being always greedy for more.

This attitude is similar to that of Lot, who gazed in greed after the prosperity of the cities of the plain (Gen. 13:10). This greed makes people easy prey for powerful figures who want to control the courts with their money.

Verse 25 seems to have nothing to do with the nearby verses except that the word *fool* appears in the Hebrew of both verses 24 and 25. Verse 21, however, is also a proverb about how a foolish son grieves his parents, and it also seems to be deliberately placed in a context that does not focus on family life. Again, the implied point may be that we should take care not to raise "foolish" children who are easily susceptible to greed and who add to the injustice and corruption of society.

APPROPRIATE USE OF WORDS (17:27–18:4)

Two proverbs bracket this collection: 17:27 declares that the wise man uses words with restraint, and 18:4 indicates that the wise man's words are profound (like deep water) and refreshing (like a bubbling brook). Also, 17:28 and 18:2 are closely related. The former says that even a fool seems intelligent if he will stay quiet, and the latter says that this is the one thing that a fool can never do. Verbosity is the mark of a fool. Finally, 18:1 and 18:3 also relate to one another. Proverbs 18:1 should be translated, "A schismatic person seeks an opportunity for a quarrel; he rails against all sound policy." Proverbs 18:3 begins, "When a base man comes, so does contempt." Both verses speak of contemptible, divisive people who throw a situation into chaos with their harangues.

Our words show us for what we are. If we speak carefully, with great significance, we are profound. If we are long-winded and highly opinionated and are constantly getting into quarrels, we are fools.

MORE PROVERBS ON EVIL SPEECH (18:5–8)

Proverbs 18:6, 7 is almost identical in meaning; it is also notable that together these verses have the sequence: "A fool's lips . . . his mouth . . . a fool's mouth . . . his lips." It is the fool's mouth, more than anything else, that gets him into deep trouble. Verse 8 also deals with speech, in that it focuses on how much people enjoy gossip. Verse 5, of itself, appears to have nothing to do with speech. In fact, however, there may be a connection to the other proverbs. People are partial to the wicked and thrust aside the rights of the innocent when they pay heed to perverse and deceptive arguments in court. Heeding gossip in society is similar to heeding false testimony and slippery arguments in courts of law.

SECURITY (18:9–12)

These four proverbs deal with personal security in one form or another. Verse 9 asserts that laziness is a form of vandalism, since laziness brings about the destruction of property as surely as the vandal does. In short, one cannot be lazy and have financial security. Verse 10 provides an apt contrast to verse 11. The Lord, not money, is true security in life. Verse 12 is somewhat paradoxical. Those who think themselves mighty and secure are those who are ready to fall, but those who have a realistic view of themselves are most secure.

ANSWERING TOO QUICK (18:13)

Answering before listening is another form of the verbose, highly opinionated habit of speech that characterizes the fool.

A BROKEN SPIRIT (18:14)

One's attitude is the most important factor in determining the well-being of a person.

JUSTICE AND THE COURTS (18:15–19)

These proverbs are rules of jurisprudence for the ancient law courts of Israel. Although verse 15 could apply to many situations, here it refers to the juror who is not satisfied with the superficial presentation of a case or one swayed by emotion; but who instead carefully seeks the facts before giving his verdict. Verse 16 does not approve of the giving of gifts and bribes; it simply asserts that it is often done and that it often works. A wise juror would want to know if a party in a suit had the support of some official because he had made a bribe.

Verse 17 warns the juror not to accept the first argument he hears. Verse 18 seems strange to modern, Western readers, but in ancient Israel the settling of disputes through casting lots was not uncommon. Verse 19 warns that out-of-court settlements are sometimes impossible and that legal disputes must be resolved through legal means. Otherwise, more conflict will follow and the situation could get out of control.

Fairness should be a basic quality of the person who knows God and who has learned right from wrong. This person will seek to settle disputes impartially and on the basis of the facts.

THE POWER OF WORDS (18:20–21)

It is difficult to know what to make of 18:20, and opinions vary. The verse could mean that a person can get his food (i.e., his income) from how he uses his words. It could be taken metaphorically to mean that people get good results from what they say. On the other hand, one could take it metaphorically to mean that people tend to feel self-satisfied in their words. That is, people get satisfaction from the feeling that they have said something powerful or profound. In this connection, verse 21 warns us that our words can have a devastating effect on people.

DIVERSE TEACHINGS I (18:22–19:14)

This text is bracketed by sayings that emphasize the importance of having a good wife and harmonious family (18:22; 19:13, 14). Between these two are a number of verses that describe various topics, although there is something of an emphasis on the poor and their plight (18:23, 24; 9:1, 3, 4, 6, 7).

Proverbs 18:22 states the general truth that a good wife is a prized possession, a gift from God. Proverbs 19:13, 14 answers this with the warning that a bad son or wife is destructive to the household. One should not imagine that a contentious wife is irritating like a leaky faucet, something that the ancient Israelites never experienced. Rather, she is like a leaking roof; more than an irritation, she is a source of damage to the house. She is not only contentious with her husband but also with people in society, and the result is that she causes a great deal of trouble for her husband. It is significant that so many proverbs between 18:22 and 19:14 focus on poverty; the point is that irresponsible family members will drive one to poverty.

Although the Bible speaks of God's compassion for the poor, it never glorifies poverty. Many proverbs here speak of the manifold suffering that poverty generates. Also, it is true that poverty with integrity is better than riches (19:1). On the other hand, when people by their own folly fall into poverty, they also lose their judgment, because they rage against God over the troubles they have brought on themselves (19:3). The poor man begs for an extension on his loan or for alms, but he is treated like a dog (18:23). Most of his friends will abandon him in time of need, although there may be one who stays by (18:24; 19:4, 7).

By contrast, people are ready to lavish attention on someone who has money and is willing to part with it (19:6). There may be an even more nefarious meaning to 19:6 in this context: People are willing to perjure themselves and pervert justice for bribes (19:5, 9). Thus, the poor man cannot get justice in the courts. It is true that God will ultimately punish such evildoers, but this does not make the plight of the poor any better.

Proverbs gives a great deal of attention to how prudence leads to a prosperous life because poverty can be so damaging and humiliating. This does not mean that the rich are assumed to be righteous and the poor evil. But we should recognize that poverty can destroy our lives and seek to follow biblical wisdom—not in order to become rich but in order to be free of the clutches of poverty and the power of the rich.

DIVERSE TEACHINGS II (19:15–20:4)

Two proverbs on laziness bracket this text (19:15; 20:4). A third proverb on laziness in the middle of the text (19:24) describes the sluggard as hopeless in his laziness. Between 19:15 and 19:24 is a text that has the following structure:

A: Obeying the commandments gives life (19:16).
  B: Give to the poor (19:17).
    C: Discipline your son (19:18).
    C': Let unrestrained people bear their punishment (19:19).
      D: Submit to instruction (19:20).
      D': Submit to the will of God (19:21).
  B': It is better to be poor than a liar (19:22).
A': The fear of the Lord gives peace (19:23).

As a whole, these proverbs deal with the need for a disciplined life and the fear of God. Instruction and the commandments (vv. 16, 20) stand alongside submission to God (vv. 21, 23) as the keys to a good life. Disciplining one's son corresponds to allowing others to bear the consequences of their actions. People must learn the lesson that actions have repercussions. On the other hand, one should show compassion to the poor rather than upbraid them for their condition. In fact, by giving to the poor, one has God for a debtor (19:17).

We may understand "mockery" here to refer to rejection of wisdom, authority, and propriety.

Proverbs 19:25–20:3, a text that falls between the second two proverbs on the sluggard (19:24; 20:4), generally focuses on the idea of mockery. Proverbs 19:25 and 29 assert that mockers receive beatings for their behavior, and 20:2 adds that the fury of a king (i.e., an authority figure) is ferocious. The ultimate form of mockery—rejection of authority—is to assault one's parents (19:26). Proverbs 19:27 is sarcastic; it should be translated, "Stop listening to instruction, my son, so that you may wander from intelligent words!" This tone is appropriate for addressing a mocker.

Proverbs 19:28 adds that a perjured witness mocks at justice and 20:1 calls wine a "mocker." It appears that the point is that undisciplined people tend to consume large amounts of alcohol and that the alcohol makes them even more obnoxious and resistant to authority. Furthermore, alcohol promotes strife. A quarrelsome personality is another characteristic of the mocker (20:3).

■ *Laziness, rejection of authority, brawling,*
■ *and abusing alcohol are qualities of the*
■ *"mocker," the person who cannot accept*
■ *authority. While these verses superficially*
■ *have nothing to do with each other, together*
■ *they form a compelling portrait of a dis-*
■ *turbed personality type.*

QUESTIONS TO GUIDE YOUR STUDY

1. How does a wise person and a fool differ in the way they make decisions?
2. Why is pride especially dangerous to those in leadership?
3. What are some of the views of laziness we get from Proverbs?

VARIOUS PROVERBS (20:5–21:8)

This large collection of proverbs generally focuses on discriminating between people of good character and people of evil character. Proverbs 20:5; 21:8 bracket this text. The former warns us that people are not what they seem and that we must exercise discernment. The latter gives the most basic principle of discernment: The wicked follow an evil way of life and the good live an upright life. This seems to be a self-evident truism, but it closes a section on discernment by advising the reader that for the most part it is not all that hard to tell the good from the bad. Between these two verses are four major sections: 20:5–12; 20:13–21; 20:22–21:3; and 21:4–7.

Discernment and Integrity (20:5–12)

The point of 20:5 is not that all people are "deep" in the sense of being profound but that their inner motives and true dispositions are well concealed. Proverbs 20:6 sounds cynical, as though honest people were impossible to find. This must be set alongside 20:7, which indicates that people of integrity do exist and that they give a wonderful heritage to their families. Proverbs 20:8 speaks of discernment on the highest level, that of a ruler dispensing justice, and verse 9 introduces an element of humility into the topic. We cannot judge others harshly when we recognize our own faults.

Being discerning is not the same as being judgmental. A familiar proverb on how God hates dishonest measures (tools for defrauding people) becomes in this context a metaphor for God's disdain for all hypocrisy and for how the wise must show discernment in their business dealings (20:10). Similarly, the fact that a child is know by his behavior (20:11) implies that the same is true for adults. Actions speak louder than words. Verse 12 reminds us that God made the eyes and ears and here it has two implications. First, we should use the tools of discernment that God has given us. Second, He who made these means of discernment will not be fooled by anyone's hypocrisy.

Various Proverbs (20:13–21)

These proverbs do not relate to one another in a special way. Proverbs 20:13, a general proverb on laziness, perhaps means that we should be diligent in practicing discernment. It is probably not accidental that after the previous verse has told us that God made the eye, this verse tells us to open our eyes.

Discernment should not be equated with a judgmental spirit. Humility before God demands that we avoid a self-righteous attitude; and charity demands that we give others the benefit of the doubt. But we will allow unworthy people to do much damage to our churches, our places of work, and our families if we do not exercise discernment.

People often say whatever is to their advantage at the moment; their true feelings can be hard to discern (20:14). Someone who speaks with wisdom is a rare jewel; we should highly value such a person. By contrast, we should avoid business dealings with someone who lacks prudence in handling money (20:16). The confidence man is a special case that calls for discernment. Proverbs 20:17 assures us that although they initially enjoy money gained through falsehood, their gains will eventually be bitter to them. A high level of discernment and a careful choosing of advisers is necessary in making major decisions, such as the decision to wage war (20:18).

Proverbs 20:19 warns us not to reveal our intentions to a gossip. Those who dishonor parents are regarded as reprobates (20:20). Proverbs 20:21 implies that we should be wary in dealing with people who acquired their money too easily. Overall, it is difficult to see any specific structure in this text, but it can be read as a series of examples that call for keen discrimination.

Dealing with the King and with the Lord (20:22–21:3)

This text appears to focus on the two judges who hold sway over people, the Lord and the king. Proverbs 20:22–25, 27, and 21:2–3 deal with divine justice, while 20:26, 28, 30 focus on royal justice. Proverbs 20:29 does not seem to fit this context, but there may be a connection nevertheless.

Proverbs 20:22 asserts that we must await justice from God and not take matters into our own hands. The next verse, 23, repeats the common maxim that God hates dishonest measures. The point may be that God will judge crooked merchants even when the victims do not know that they have been defrauded. Verse 24 adds the observation that divine control of events is far more pervasive than we realize. It should be translated, "A man's steps are guided by the Lord, but how shall a human understand God's ways?" The message appears to be that God's justice is operating even when we do not see or comprehend it. Verse 25 moves in a slightly different direction: God is your judge, so do not be thoughtless in dealing with him.

Verse 27 is difficult in the Hebrew but can be translated, "Human breath is the Lord's lamp, searching the inner chambers of the heart." The idea is that God breathed the breath of life into Adam at creation (Gen. 2:7) and that this light shines inside of people like a lamp. It illumines their thoughts, motives, and desires. Thus, no thoughts are hidden from God.

The king dispenses justice. Proverbs 20:26 asserts that it is in his interest and the interest of the country for him to punish evildoers severely. Sometimes he must use the lash to convince evildoers that crime does not pay (20:30). At the same time, his power cannot rest on brute force. He needs to foster a spirit of kindness and loyalty among his subjects (20:28).

The final judge is God and not the king (21:1–3). In fact, God even controls the king (v. 1). This does not mean that every king is just or that all his actions are good; it means that royal power is simply another of God's tools for governing the world. Verse 2 carries divine justice to a new level: God not only sees through those who fool others; he even sees through those who fooled themselves. Verse 3 warns the reader that when dealing with God, it is best not to try to fool Him with an external show of piety. It is better simply to do the right thing.

Proverbs 20:29 is distinctive among these verses because it has nothing to do with divine or royal government. On the other hand, the text may imply that young men tend to rule by strength alone while older men know that one must rule with wisdom and restraint.

The Devices and the Decline of the Wicked (21:4–8)

The teachings on discernment close with a warning about what will happen to the wicked. Verse 4 is remarkable for calling haughtiness the "lamp of the wicked." What wisdom and the Word of God are to the righteous, pride and selfishness are to the wicked. They live by the light of their arrogance. Verses 5–7 tell how fraud and the violence of the wicked, the means by which they seek quick money, drag them to poverty and death. Verse 8 aptly summarizes all of 20:5–21:8. The wicked are those who do evil. A person who recognizes this simple fact will be on the way to wisdom.

Rehoboam is a prime example of a king who attempted to rule by strength alone (1 Kings 12).

UNDER ONE ROOF (21:9–19)

The verses in this text discus four distinct concepts arranged in a chiasmus.

A: The quarrelsome wife (v. 9)
   B: On Retribution (vv. 10–13)
      C: On gifts and justice (vv. 14–15)
   B´: On Retribution (vv. 16–18)
A´: The quarrelsome wife (v. 19)

Verses 9 and 19 assert that any situation is better than living with a quarrelsome wife. Verses 10–13 are themselves a small chiasmus: They describe merciless behavior and the retribution it receives, while verses 11, 12 assert that people can observe the punishment that comes on the wicked and learn some valuable lessons. Verse 12 should be translated, "A righteous man observes the house of the wicked, how wickedness brings it to ruin."

Verses 16–18 declare that people will get what they deserve. Those who stray from the right way will die (v. 16), those who love pleasure will suffer the pains of want and poverty (v. 17), and God will take the punishment that the righteous deserve and heap it on the wicked (v. 18). Verse 18 should not be taken literally, as though the righteous were never punished for their own sins or as though the wicked really did provide an atonement for sin. The verse simply states very emphatically that the wicked will suffer for their wickedness.

The verses tell us to appease an opponent with gifts if possible and appropriate, but they also remind us that bribes in matters of criminal justice are very corrupting.

The "gift" of verse 14 could be a peace offering meant to appease an adversary, similar to the modern practice of settling out of court. The fact that it is given "in secret" does not necessarily have an evil connotation; even today, out-of-court settlements are often kept secret. On the other hand, the "gift" could be a bribe, and verse 15 reminds us that society can function well only if justice is carried out.

■ *It is curious that sayings about a quarrel-*
■ *some wife bracket these verses. It is possible*
■ *that there is a reason for this arrangement.*
■ *Proverbs 31:10–31 teaches the young man*
■ *that his success in life depends to a great*
■ *degree on the qualities of his wife. Much of*
■ *the behavior in this passage focuses on*
■ *greed (e.g., indifference to the poor [v. 13],*
■ *bribery [v. 14], and loving pleasure [v.*
■ *17]). The implication may be that the man*
■ *with a demanding, quarrelsome wife is*
■ *driven to this kind of behavior in order to*
■ *pacify her.*

REWARDS FOR DOING RIGHT (21:20–22)

These three verses describe the benefits of wisdom and virtue. Verse 12 should not be read to mean that wisdom makes you rich. Although it does imply a measure of prosperity (primarily because the wise do not consume all they have), in conjunction with verse 13 the real benefits of following this path are righteousness, life, and happiness. Verse 22 probably should not be taken literally as a simple assertion that brains are better than brawn. Verse 20 implies that the wise person can dwell securely with his possessions in his house, but verse 22 says that he can overthrow the strongest fortress that is set against him. The point is that he has a life that is victorious over those who live by brute force.

A MOUTH IN AND OUT OF CONTROL (21:23, 24)

These verses contrast two kinds of people: those who are careful about what they say and those who are obnoxious and boastful with their words. Unwillingness to curb one's words is a sign of pride.

THE SLUGGARD'S CRAVING (21:25–26)

Proverbs frequently attacks or mocks the behavior of the lazy, but it does more than just endorse a strong work ethic. It also demands compassion from people.

TRYING TO FOOL GOD (21:27)

An outward show of piety from an unrepentant heart does not fool God. The text does not tell us what the "evil intent" of this person is. It could be a show of hypocritical devotion, an attempt to buy God's support for a selfish plan, or desire to assuage a guilty conscience without repenting.

THE FALSE WITNESS (21:28, 29)

These two verses should be rendered, "A false witness will perish, and whoever listens to him will be driven out forever. A wicked man puts up a bold front, but the just man understands the wicked man's ways." Verse 28 teaches that punishment awaits both the perjurer ("false witness") and the gullible or corrupt juror ("whoever listens to him") who carelessly accepts the perjurer's testimony. Verse 29 adds that although the perjurer lies boldly, the righteous man can see through it.

COUNTER WISDOM (21:30, 31)

In Proverbs, "wisdom" almost always includes prudence in daily life ("common sense"), skill in leadership, personal integrity, and the fear of

God. By contrast, Proverbs generally regards the kind of intelligence that is without moral guidance and the fear of God as a kind of cunning, not as true wisdom. Here, "wisdom" (including military skills) that is without the fear of God is bound to fail. Intelligence without godliness is another form of folly.

A GOOD NAME (22:1)

Wealth is not bad, but if it comes at the expense of the respect of the community, it is too costly. This proverb seems to be a prologue to the following text.

WEALTH, POVERTY, AND A PRUDENT LIFE (22:2–5)

These four verses have a parallel structure, as follows:

A: Rich and poor equal before the Lord (v. 2)
   B: How the wise and the fool face the dangers of life (v. 3)
A´: Riches come from fear of the Lord (v. 4)
   B´: How the upright and the wicked face the dangers of life (v. 5)

We generally get into trouble because we acted without thinking, because we refused to listen to good advice, and because we didn't act on the basis of the fear of God.

Verse 2, in this context, does not deal with the duty of the rich to be compassionate toward the poor so much as it reminds them that they also depend wholly upon God (contrast 29:13, where the same proverb appears in a different context). This leads into verse 4, which reminds us that a person obtains prosperity and happiness in life through the fear of God.

Verses 3 and 5 indicate that people stumble into danger because they are headstrong, unwilling to listen, and evil in their selfishness. The dangers into which they fall may be economic, physical, or moral. A life of prudence and true piety leads to security.

VARIOUS PROVERBS (22:6–16)

The proverbs of this text are somewhat miscellaneous in order, but verses 6, 7 and verses 15, 16 appear to bracket the text in an inclusion structure. Verses 6 and 15 focus on the training of children and verses 7 and 16 deal with the power the rich have over the poor.

Verse 6 is one of the best known proverbs of the Bible; unfortunately, the translation and meaning of the verse are much disputed. A good case can be made for rendering it, "Train up a child in a manner befitting a child, and as he grows old he will not depart from it." The proverb does not mean that if one gives a child instruction in the truth during his childhood that he will return to that teaching in later years after a period of rebellion. Nor does it mean that one should train up a child "according to his or her own nature," as though the point were that one should tailor training to the individual personality of every child (there may be truth in that, but it is not the point of this verse).

Christian nurture, the education of small children in the things of God, is a fundamental duty of Christian families and of the church. But this nurture must be appropriate to the psychological development, intellectual comprehension, and moral consciousness of small children.

Rather, the idea is that if parents begin by teaching small children in the ways of God on a level that they can understand and increase the sophistication of the teaching as the child grows, it is much more likely that the child will remain steadfast in the truth.

Verse 15 looks at the other side of childhood nurture—the need for discipline. Just as children cannot be taught on an adult level, neither can they be reasoned with on an adult level. They must receive punishment or discipline appropriate for their age.

Verses 7 and 16 look at the power the rich have over the poor, but verse 16 describes those who oppress the poor while the poor try to ingratiate themselves with the rich by giving them gifts. Verse 7 states the fact that the rich control the lives of the poor. By implication, it tells us that we should avoid falling into poverty because it takes away our control over our lives. It is precisely for this reason that the wise try to stay out of debt.

Verses 8, 9 maintain the familiar biblical teaching that you reap what you sow. Verse 9, however, adds a new dimension: You should share the benefits of a good harvest with the poor. The Bible adds compassion to what might otherwise be a harsh, unyielding doctrine.

Verses 11–14 describe five ways that people use words. The "mocker" stirs up strife and must be expelled from the community (v. 10). The pure in heart speak the truth with tact and are received even by kings (v. 11)—a clear contrast to what happens to the mocker. The faithless use words to pervert the truth, but God will show them to be the fools that they are (v. 12). The sluggard uses words to make outrageous excuses for his failure to do any work (v. 13). Finally, the prostitute uses her mouth to seduce the young man and drag him down to the grave (v. 14).

THE THIRTY SAYINGS (22:17–24:22)

This text belongs to the collection of Solomon (1:1–24:34), but it is similar to an Egyptian collection of sayings called the teachings of Amenemope. This is a piece of Egyptian wisdom literature that was written before the time of Solomon. Like this text, it is a set of thirty teachings, and although there are differences, there are some similarities between the two that are too close to be explained as coincidence. The simplest explanation is that Solomon knew of this

Israelite wisdom literature reflects awareness of the great literature of the ancient world. Song of Songs has striking resemblances to the love poetry of ancient Egypt, for example, and Ecclesiastes has material that is similar to poetry found in the epic of Gilgamesh. In all these examples, the non-Israelite literature is older than the biblical counterparts.

wisdom, made use of its format, and included a few of its teaching with significant modifications. One should not be surprised that a book of the Bible reflects the culture and literature of its day; it would be most surprising if it did not.

Introduction (22:17–21)

In a typical prologue, the introduction declares that the teaching that follows will guide one in understanding and in the fear of God. Verse 20 is somewhat difficult in the Hebrew, but it should be translated, "Have I not written for you thirty sayings of counsel and understanding?"

Saying 1 (22:22, 23)

Ancient wisdom literature often spoke of the need to maintain the rights of the poor, but the Israelite version adds the motivation that the Lord is watching out for the poor. The point is that God would (1) take up the case of the poor as their legal advocate and (2) plunder the plunderers of the poor in recompense for their actions.

Saying 2 (22:24, 25)

This saying is a simple warning to avoid bad company, but the end of verse 25 could be rendered, "And (lest) you take bait to your soul." The idea may be that wicked companions offer the bait of easy money and companionship to the gullible young men but in the process get their hooks into his soul.

Saying 3 (22:26, 27)

A person should not put his or her savings at risk.

Wisdom includes financial prudence. The point of this passage is that those who put up their possessions as security for a loan for a friend are likely to have everything, including the mats they sleep on, seized by a creditor.

Saying 4 (22:28)

Moving a boundary stone was a clandestine way to steal property. In an Israelite context, however, it also had the effect of nullifying the heritage of land that the ancestors of Israel had established for the nation (see Josh. 13–22).

Saying 5 (22:29)

Quality work, in any field, will get the recognition it deserves.

Saying 6 (23:1–3)

Beware of taking favors from rich and powerful people. They generally want something in exchange, and their price can be very high. To put a knife to one's own throat is to take extreme precautions against overindulgence.

Saying 7 (23:4, 5)

A person should not make becoming rich his or her goal in life. Like a donkey chasing a carrot on a stick, wealth continually pulls away from us. Proverbs advises us on how to have a prosperous life without offering the empty promise that it will make us rich.

Saying 8 (23:6–8)

Just as we should not make riches the goal of our lives, so we should not cultivate the favor of the rich. Following the translation found in the Septuagint, verse 7 may be translated as, "For like a hair in the throat, so he is." The point is that when the rich man gives, he always has some insidious means of getting back what he has given. Just as a person feels a hair in his mouth with a bite of food and suddenly gags, so those who take from the rich suddenly find themselves giving it all back in a very unhappy manner.

Saying 9 (23:9)

It is hopeless to give pearls of wisdom to ethical swine. To put this saying in theological terms, people must repent before many of the teachings of the Bible will have any meaning for them.

Saying 10 (23:10, 11)

To move boundary stones or take the land of the fatherless is to seize property from those who cannot resist. God, however, will defend them, and his vengeance on the evildoer can be very severe.

Saying 11 (23:12)

This verse declares that one keeps on learning, especially in the ways of God, through all of life.

The raising of children involves the giving of both punishment (saying number 12) and praise (saying number 13). To do one without the other is to give a child an unbalanced upbringing.

Saying 12 (23:13, 14)

Disciplining a child is a means of shaping his character so that he does not fall into self-destructive habits or fail to learn to accept authority. This does not justify brutalizing a child.

Saying 13 (23:15, 16)

Children should understand that when they do right, it gives great joy to parents; this serves as an added incentive for children to do right. It also implies that praise, and not just punishment, is a means of training a child.

Saying 14 (23:17, 18)

Parents fear that their teaching will be undermined by peers and bad role models, and thus this text advises the son not to envy sinners. Verse 18 could be translated, "For if you maintain the fear of the Lord, you will have a future, and your hope will not be cut off."

Saying 15 (23:19–21)

This text condemns both drunkenness and gluttony. Many Christians avoid the former but embrace the latter. Both are destructive, indicating that a person is controlled by appetites.

Saying 16 (23:22–25)

Some interpreters regard the "father" figure of Proverbs as representing the teacher and not necessarily the literal father of the young man, but the fact that the text mentions both father and mother indicates that actual parents are meant here. The admonition to the young man not to despise his mother when she is old does not mean that his parents are old, only that he perceives them that way. A "generation gap" can occur even in very traditional cultures.

Saying 17 (23:26–28)

Once again, parents plead with their son to stay away from the prostitute. She is a deep pit from whom the young man cannot escape and a robber who wants to take all he has. She "increases the faithless among men" (NASB), in the sense that she helps promote decadence in society and infidelity among husbands toward their wives.

Saying 18 (23:29–35)

With profound pathos (and a little sarcasm), this text depicts the woes of those who abuse alcohol (and in modern society, drugs as well). The sparkling of the wine describes its attractiveness; as with the allure of the prostitute, it offers pleasures that many people find tempting. But a person pays for those pleasures with sickness, delirium, and incapacitation.

Saying 19 (24:1, 2)

Admonitions not to envy the wicked often contain assurance that the wicked will soon perish or suffer the wrath of God (cp. Prov. 3:31–33). In

All forms of substance abuse (whether alcohol, prescription drugs, or illegal narcotics) offer brief pleasure while destroying body, mind, and spirit. This is a classic example of how wisdom demands that we live in accordance with the rules God has built into creation. Our bodies were not made to withstand that kind of artificial stimulation or euphoria.

this text, however, the reason a person should not envy them is simply that they are corrupt.

Saying 20 (24:3, 4)

The "riches" that fill the house of the righteous could be literal or metaphorical, but they are probably metaphorical and refer to a joyful, healthy household.

Saying 21 (24:5, 6)

Only a king or ruler could fulfill this text since ordinary people do not wage wars. Probably we should read this metaphorically to mean that by wisdom we will have victory in the conflicts and struggles of life.

Saying 22 (24:7)

This can be translated, "Wisdom is too high for a fool, let him not open his mouth in the gate." The point is that "fools" have nothing to contribute to important discussions.

Saying 23 (24:8, 9)

Those who scheme and devise mischief will get a reputation for being devious. A bad reputation is not easily overcome.

Saying 24 (24:10)

Everyone faces trials in life, and these trials reveal whether a person has strong character. This text speaks of failing the tests of life in order to encourage us not to fail.

Saying 25 (24:11, 12)

The slaughter of Jews in the Holocaust is a powerful example of a situation in which decent people should have come to the rescue of the prisoners. Pleas of ignorance do not impress God. It is striking that this teaching comes immediately after 24:10, which exhorts us to be strong in the day of trouble.

Saying 26 (24:13, 14)

There is a common notion that whatever is good for you must be unpleasant and that God disapproves of all forms of fun. Here, the father calls on his son to embrace wisdom because it makes life pleasant, like the eating of honey.

Saying 27 (24:15, 16)

Verse 15 should be rendered, "Do not lie in ambush, O outlaw, against a righteous man's estate!" This is ironic advice to the wicked, implying that they should not even try starting a fight with the righteous. The righteous person is so resilient that the wicked cannot win.

Saying 28 (24:17, 18)

It is curious that we are told to refrain from gloating over the fall of an enemy because, otherwise, God might see our gloating and stop afflicting our enemy. It seems that our purpose in not gloating is to further the suffering of the enemy! In fact, however, the practice of not gloating trains us in the art of forgiveness.

One result of learning biblical wisdom is that we become mature people. A person of character does not rejoice over the suffering of enemies, tells the truth, lives within his means, is generous but is not sucked into throwing away his money, and can love faithfully. Biblical wisdom makes us more *human.*

Saying 29 (24:19, 20)

Those who are truly mature in wisdom and faith can have peace even in a world filled with evil. Those who understand that this world is broken but that God will set all wrongs right can have tranquility without losing any sense of indignation over deeds of wickedness.

Saying 30 (24:21, 22)

Verse 21 is difficult in the Hebrew, but it should probably be translated, "Fear the Lord and the king, my son, and do not rebel against either." The point is that the son must learn to accept both human and divine authority if he is to succeed in life.

- *The thirty sayings of 22:17–24:22 cover a*
- *wide range of topics, including wise use of*
- *money, compassion for the poor, the dangers*
- *of the prostitute, the training of children,*
- *drunkenness, and submission to God. It often*
- *speaks from a father's point of view. It is, in*
- *effect, a miniature book of Proverbs in that it*
- *covers most of the topics which the larger*
- *book addresses.*

QUESTIONS TO GUIDE YOUR STUDY

1. Why do we need to be careful in choosing advisors?
2. What are the practical implications of God's being omniscient?
3. What are God's promises to parents as they raise their children?

PROVERBS 24:23–31:31

ON THE COURTS AND LAZINESS (24:23, 34)

This is a text of four sayings arranged in a parallel fashion, as follows:

A: On the law courts (vv. 23–26)

   B: On work (v. 27)

A´: On the law courts (vv. 28, 29)

   B´: On laziness (vv. 30–34)

Verses 23–26 assert that a person must not show favoritism or pervert justice in legal proceedings. Verse 26 should probably be translated, "He who gives a proper verdict silences hostile lips." Verse 27 states that a person should first provide a means of income (work in the fields) and only afterward provide for personal comfort (build a house). Verses 28, 29 describe the role of a witness in court just as verses 23–26 describe the role of the judge or jury. The obvious point is that one should not commit perjury. Verses 30–34 go back to the issue of work, here with an emphasis on laziness. The fields of the sluggard were in disrepair, his property had declined in value, and he had no income from his vineyard.

■ *Proper conduct in courts of law and diligence*
■ *about doing one's work seem to have little to*
■ *do with each other, but here they are woven*
■ *together. One should not try to force an arti-*
■ *ficial connection between the two spheres of*
■ *activity, but understand the biblical wisdom*
■ *seeks to train us in every area of life because*
■ *a serious flaw in any one of these areas can*
■ *have disastrous consequences.*

THE BOOK OF HEZEKIAH (25:1–29:27)

As described in the introduction, chapters 25–29 are a separate collection of sayings collected and edited by the scribes of Hezekiah. It only has a title and a main body of instruction without subheadings or a prologue.

Hezekiah ruled Judah 716–686 B.C. Matthew lists Hezekiah in the genealogy of Jesus. (Matt. 1:9–10).

On Dealing with Kings (25:2–7)

This text is highly respectful of royal authority and it may have been composed by the "men of Hezekiah" as a tribute to the two great scholar-kings of Israel, Solomon and Hezekiah. One should have high respect for the office of king and behave accordingly. In addition, the highest service a person can render to a ruler is to work to ensure that justice—not corruption prevails throughout the administration. Verse 7 is somewhat difficult in the Hebrew; it should be translated, "It is good that he say to you, 'Come up here!' rather than that you be demoted in the presence of a noble whom your eyes see."

Settling Disputes without Litigation (25:8–10)

The grammar of this passage is somewhat difficult because the speaker interrupts himself in a device technically known as anacoluthon. It can be translated as follows: "Do not take a matter to litigation quickly, lest—what will you do afterwards, when your adversary humiliates you? Make your case to your adversary and do not reveal it to another arbitrator, lest when he hears it he finds against you, and there be no end to your disgrace." The point is very simple: Try to settle disputes out of court!

Fine Jewelry and Fine Counsel (25:11, 12)

These two proverbs refer to the importance of giving good counsel. The proverbs compare good advice to fine jewelry. It is possible that verse 11a means, "A word spoken in its two lines." If so, the "two lines" are the two lines of a proverb.

Reliable and Unreliable People (25:13, 14)

These two proverbs use similes from agricultural life to describe the importance of being a reliable person. Snow at harvesttime does not mean that it snows on the fields, which would be a disaster. It refers to snow brought down from the mountains which gives refreshment to workers out in the fields. Clouds without rain are empty promises that give only disappointment. Those whom one can trust to do their jobs are refreshing; those who promise

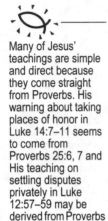

Many of Jesus' teachings are simple and direct because they come straight from Proverbs. His warning about taking places of honor in Luke 14:7–11 seems to come from Proverbs 25:6, 7 and His teaching on settling disputes privately in Luke 12:57–59 may be derived from Proverbs 25:8–10.

big things but do not deliver leave people feeling cheated.

Be Patient with the Authorities (25:15)

Bones are the most rigid parts of the human body. Rigid people in authority can often be persuaded by gentleness where bluster and demands fail.

Enough Is Enough (25:16, 17)

Here, the dietary proverb of verse 16 serves as the metaphor for the social proverb of verse 17. In a general sense, this text warns us against every kind of excess, but the focus is on dealing with other people. One must learn to avoid becoming a nuisance to friends. This requires that we understand the disposition of the other person and the nature of the relationship with that person.

Personal character is at the heart of the teachings of Proverbs. It warns us about the kinds of people to avoid and the kinds of traits to eradicate in ourselves. Integrity, good social skills, and strong character are not optional in the Christian life.

Beware of These People (25:18–20)

These three proverbs give colorful metaphors for people whom one would do well to avoid. Perjurers (v. 18) are obviously extremely dangerous; no one should enter into a relationship with such a person. Unreliable people (v. 19) are like bad teeth in that they hurt you when you need them. People who "sing songs to a heavy heart" (v. 20) are oblivious to the emotional state of others. These people are apt to give someone a jolt when they need it least.

Strange but True (25:21, 22)

This proverb states the paradoxical truth that the best way to get ahead of your enemy is to show compassion toward him or her. The proverb does not deal with the possibility of reconciliation, although of course that can happen. The idea seems to be that having to take food from an enemy is humiliating, and that God rewards the person who gives the food. Paul cites this text in Romans 12:20.

Cold Rain and Cold Looks (25:23)
A problem with this proverb is that in Israel, the north wind does not bring rain. The proverb may have come from Egypt, where rains came out of the north and were often unwelcome. The Hebrew is also difficult. It could be translated, "As a cold wind gives birth to rains, so cold looks give birth to a storm of slander." The idea seems to be that cold stares and lack of communication give rise to gossip and slander.

A Nagging Wife (25:24)
This proverb occurs also in 21:9. The meaning, obviously enough, is that a nagging wife makes home life miserable.

Good Water and Bad Water (25:25, 26)
These two proverbs are linked by the common idea of drinking water. In the first, good news from a distant land is refreshing. This may be a good report on a distant business transaction, or it may simply be good news that was altogether unexpected. By contrast, when a righteous person yields to evil, he is a disappointment to others. People depend upon the integrity of the righteous the same way desert travelers depend on springs at oases.

Sweets for the Body and Sweets for the Mind (25:27)
Verse 27a looks back to verse 16, which also deals with eating honey in excess. But the translation of 27b is difficult. It could mean, "But seeking out difficult things is glorious." This seems like an odd second line, but it may look back to verse 2, which asserts that it is glory for kings to search out difficult matters. If so, then this verse closes off a section of the

Sometimes believers fail to do right not because they are personally immoral but because they lack the backbone to stand up against evil. Courage and resolution to do the right are as much a part of the character of Christ as is private morality.

Hezekiah text, since verse 27 acts as closure to verses 2 and 16.

Portrait of a Fool (25:28–26:12)

The reader does well to remember that the "fool" of Proverbs is not necessarily the person who is unintelligent. The fool is someone who has rejected the counsel of wisdom and whose understanding of life is fundamentally wrong. The fools of proverbs are generally arrogant, scheming, and self-centered.

This text is in several parts. First, in 25:28–26:2, we have three similes on the actions of fools. They are defenseless in life not because they are weak but because they lack self-control (25:28). Giving a fool honor is inappropriate and ultimately destructive (26:1). Rain was highly treasured in ancient Israel, but if it came at the wrong time it could do much damage. In the same way, a fool who gets honor is likely to take responsibility that he cannot handle. When fools insult people it does no good, because everyone knows what the source is (26:2).

Verses 3–5 all concern the appropriate way to correct a fool. According to verse 3, the whip is the only reproof they actually understand. Verses 4 and 5 seem to contradict each other. They first deny and then affirm that one should answer a fool according to his folly. But this only gives us a good example of how proverbs work. They are general truths that at times apply but that at other times do not apply. Sometimes it is wise and sometimes it is not wise to answer a fool with the same kind of heat, emotion, and invective that the fool himself uses. Sometimes a person must speak in this way to get across to fools, but those who do it too much become like the fools they deal with.

In verses 6–10 we have a chiasmus, as follows:

A: Committing important business to a fool (v. 6)
  B: A proverb in a fool's mouth (v. 7)
    C: Honor for a fool (v. 8)
  B′: A proverb in a fool's mouth (v. 9)
A′: Committing important business to a fool (v. 10)

The common thread that unites these five verses is that a person should not give a fool respect or responsibility that he does not merit. One should not entrust important business to him or suppose that his ability to cite proverbs makes him wise.

The metaphors of this passage are extremely colorful. To tie a stone in a sling (v. 8) means more than that the stone won't go anywhere; it may swing around and hit the slinger. A proverb from a fool is like lame legs in that it does not get anywhere (v. 7); it is like a thorn in a drunkard's hand in that it loses its sting (v. 9). Verse 6 may actually mean, "He cuts off his feet and bares his own bottom who sends a message by the hand of a fool." In other words, whoever entrusts important business to a fool will not only see his business fail but will also look ludicrous in the process.

"Cutting off one's feet" means that the message will not get anywhere; to bare one's bottom is to expose oneself to public ridicule (cp. 2 Sam. 10:4).

Verses 11, 12 close off this text with two appropriate lessons: Fools do not learn from their mistakes and the quintessential fool is the person who is sure of his or her own wisdom.

■ *This text gives us an extended picture of a*
■ *fool, a person who is unreliable, unteachable,*
■ *and arrogant. This prepares the way for*
■ *three other portraits: the sluggard*
■ *(26:13–16), the busybody (26:17–22), and*
■ *the liar (26:23–28). Proverbs 26 gives us*
■ *complete portrayals of the kinds of people*
■ *that wise people should avoid.*

Portrait of a Sluggard (26:13–16)

The sluggard has four characteristics. First, any excuse, no matter how outlandish, is for him a good reason to stay in and not go to work (v. 13). Second, his "activity" of choice is turning in his bed (v. 14). Third, he is too lazy even to do things that benefit him directly (v. 15). Fourth, he thinks his ability to shun work is the mark of true wisdom (v. 16).

Portrait of a Busybody (26:17–22)

These verses describe the person who meddles in the quarrels of others, who spreads rumor and falsehood, who keeps a dispute alive by adding fuel to the fire, and who simply loves gossip. In context, verse 19 is probably not describing the ordinary practical joker or kidder but the person who spreads rumors and then claims he did not mean any harm. The whole passage asserts that one should stay out of other people's differences and above all else should do nothing to perpetuate a conflict.

Portrait of a Liar (26:23–28)

The liar is first of all a phony, like a veneer of fine glaze over a cheap, common pot. The text goes to great lengths to point out that the liar is full of hatred, malice, and abominations. A soul that is full of lies is also full of spite. Nevertheless, this kind of person will soon be exposed and trapped in his own lies. Verse 27 is a common Old Testament proverb (see Pss. 7:15; 9:15; Eccl. 10:8). Here, it has been applied to the story of the liar. He lays elaborate schemes and dangerous snares, but they only serve to entrap the liar himself.

Boasting and Praise (27:1, 2)

Most English versions say that we should not "boast" about tomorrow and let another "praise" us rather than ourselves. In Hebrew, "boast" and "praise" are from the same root. We should neither be too sure about the future nor too confident of our own gifts. Both lead to the kind of pride that precedes destruction.

Unbearable Personalities (27:3, 4)

In Hebrew, these two verses closely parallel one another and belong together. Two types of behavior that try the patience of a saint are provocation by the obnoxious and anger that comes from jealousy. Both kinds of people have warped personalities that are not open to reason.

Honest Friendship (27:5, 6)

This does not mean that it is always better to rebuke or that there is never a time when tactful silence is the wiser course. The point is that we should distinguish between true friends and false ones, and also that we should express our love and concern for others.

Behind verse 5 is the idea that in order for any kind of valid relationship to exist, there must be open communication. Love is of no value if it is not expressed. By comparison, even open rebuke can lead to a more genuine relationship. This leads to the thought of verse 6, that not all stinging rebukes come from antagonism and not all expressions of affection come from true love. A true friend will tell the truth where an enemy only flatters. Verse 6 literally says, "The wounds of a friend are faithful, but the kisses of an enemy are abundant."

Real Friends, Close at Hand (27:7–10)

These four verses have a parallel (A-B-A´-B´) pattern. Verses 7 and 9 (A and A´) deal with pleasant substances (honey, incense, and perfume) and a paradox that sometimes the bitter is preferable to the sweet. Verse 8 (B) counsels a man not to wander far from home while verse 10 (B´) counsels him to make friends with those who are near since family may be far away.

By itself, verse 7 is a fairly generic proverb about the glut which kills pleasure while hunger excites it. In connection with verse 9, however, it seems that the "honey" represents superficial friendships that seem pleasant but soon become tedious—in contrast to the "bitter" taste of a friend who offers plain, solid advice but whose help is greatly appreciated in times of trouble, when one is "hungry."

Building and maintaining close relationships with family and friends can be called the most important task of life. We need to recognize close relationships as what they are, things that are as essential to life as food and oxygen.

Verse 8 contrasts with verse 10; the former tells the reader not to wander far from home and the latter tells him to make close friendships with those around him if he is far from home and family. Here again, there is no real contradiction. The point is that we will die if we do not have a support system of people whom we can trust and turn to in time of need. "Family" is essential for life and well being.

Fatherly Advice (27:11–27)

It is quite surprising to read a text here that looks much like the parental appeals in Proverbs 1–9. Of course, one could read verse 11 as no more than an interjection, but verses 12–27 concern the kinds of things that a father would be concerned about for his son: how to follow sound business practices and how to maintain good relationships with the men in the community.

Therefore, one should take this text for what it appears to be, a true parental exhortation.

In verse 11, the father states that his son's wisdom will enable him to respond to those who hate him. A son's behavior will bring his father either honor or contempt in the community.

Simple lessons of tact and manners are very important for a young man's success in life. Such a person will know how to treat others with respect and also how to correct and rebuke another person in a fitting manner. Time spent learning social skills is not time wasted.

Verses 12, 13 deal with prudence in business (other verses in this passage that focus on fiscal responsibility are 15, 16, 18, 20, 23–27). Here, the message is that prudent people have foresight and know when to turn aside from danger. One clear example is this: Never enter an unsecured business relationship with a man who puts up security for a loose woman!

In verse 14, as in 17, 19, and 21, 22, the father teaches the son how to get along with other members of the community (especially with other men). The message of this verse is simple: Don't come across with too much bluster and bonhomie with other men (especially early in the morning!), or they will find it offensive.

It is not surprising that a father would want his son to be wise about whom he marries, and verses 15, 16 address this issue. The woman in view is quarrelsome and generally trouble for her husband. In short, this is the kind of wife the father does not want his son to choose. Verse 16 can be translated as follows, "He who keeps her keeps wind, and he will call her the perfume of his right hand." Keeping her is like keeping wind in that he cannot restrain her from spending money and making trouble. She is "perfume in the right hand" (that is, very expensive perfume) in the sense that maintaining her is like keeping up a stock of very expensive perfume. The term is an ironic term of affection. This perfume is costly but does him little good. Such a wife stands in stark contrast to the good wife of Proverbs 31:10–31.

Verse 17 encourages the young man to spend time with peers since there is no better way to be challenged to improve himself.

According to verse 18, those who do their duty will receive appropriate rewards. The translation of verse 19 is difficult, but the point appears to be that there is a correspondence between the inner and outer person. One must learn how to read people and separate the phonies from the real. Verse 20 follows this with advice that the young man be on the lookout for greedy people (death here serves as an analogy for human avarice).

Verse 21 continues the theme of learning how to read people. It should be translated, "A crucible is for silver and a smelter is for gold, but as for a man, go by his reputation." Verse 22 picks up on the analogy of smelting and shifts to an analogy of mortar and pestle, making the point that fools cannot be separated from their folly. The point is that you should avoid entangling relations with such people; it is ignorance to suppose that their ethical shortcomings will not come back to hurt you.

Verses 23–27 close this exhortation with a simple business lesson: take care of your business and your business will take care of you. The point of verse 27 is not that the whole family will live on a diet of nothing but goat's milk but that the goat's milk alone will bring in enough income to sustain the family.

> ■ *A young man needs a few basic skills as he*
> ■ *enters adult life. He must be able to get along*
> ■ *with other people, especially the men of his*
> ■ *community, and he must know how to read*
> ■ *their character. He must also know how to*
> ■ *look after his business. With these skills, he*
> ■ *will be well equipped to provide for his family.*

A Life of Fear (28:1)

Nothing gives a person boldness like a clean conscience. On the other hand, people who are full of guilt, fear of reprisal, and the sense of having made many enemies can become virtually paranoid.

The Distortions Evil Causes (28:2)

The Hebrew of this verse is difficult, but it seems to mean that when wickedness prevails in society and government, the political situation is very unstable, and many people will vie for power.

Oppression, Keeping in the Right Way, and the Law (28:3–11)

This series of verses appears to have a focus on the Law of God in a structure of two parallel texts:

A: Oppression of the poor (v. 3)
  B: Forsaking the Law (v. 4)
    C: Understanding right and wrong (v. 5)
      D: The poor can be better off than the rich (v. 6)
  B: Keeping the Law (v. 7)
A: Oppression of the poor (v. 8)
  B: Ignoring the Law (v. 9)
    C: The wrong and right paths (v. 10)
      D: The poor can be smarter than the rich (v. 11)

The passage emphasizes a distinction between the poor and the rich. The poor are often oppressed by the rich, but they can be morally superior to them as well as see through their phoniness. This passage also emphasizes a distinction between justice and the perversion of justice. The moral direction of the Law separates those who are apparently blessed by God (the rich) from those whom God truly favors (the righteous, even if they are poor).

The oppressor in verse 3 is like a driving rain. Normally rain is good for the crops, but a driving rain destroys them. In the same way, God has given some people authority so they might protect the poor. Oppressive rulers misuse that stewardship, and like the driving rain that destroys crops, they beat down the poor. The oppressor of verse 8 uses financial power to enrich himself, but God will remove the money that was entrusted to him and give it to another.

There is an interesting progression in verses 4, 7, and 9. The young man who rejects the law chooses bad companions (v. 4), becomes a glutton and disgraces his family (v. 7), and is finally detestable to God Himself (v. 9). Such a young man is likely to be the oppressive aristocrat portrayed throughout this passage.

Verse 5 speaks of knowing right from wrong, while verse 10 describes those who teach a false wisdom. An example of the kind of false wisdom this text warns against is the modern perversion of the Golden Rule: "He who has the gold makes the rules."

Verse 6 could be translated, "Better is a poor man who walks in his integrity than someone who perverts the two ways, even if he is rich." This seems to be an explicit reference to the

People with wealth and privilege have a special obligation to those who have less, but the temptation is for them to abuse their power. If, however, they receive teaching in the Bible and understand the duties God has laid upon them, they are less likely to fall into this trap.

doctrine of the two ways, the way of wisdom and the way of folly, that Proverbs always alludes to. This person perverts teaching about the two ways through clever words so that right seems wrong and wrong seems right. Verse 11 closes this section with a parallel thought, but it adds the distinctive emphasis that the righteous poor can see through the pretense of the rich.

Good Government and Bad Government I (28:12)

The end of this verse might be paraphrased, "But when the wicked come to power, it is hard to find a real man." The idea is that wicked leadership brings down all of society to a bestial level. Even people who might otherwise be decent or noble become cowardly and self-seeking.

Turning from Sin (28:13, 14)

The first line in 28:14, "Blessed is the man who always fears the LORD," is similar to Jesus' surprising way of teaching in the Beatitudes. There, as here, an attitude that at first may seem undesirable turns out to be reflective of the kind of humility that God seeks in people. Jesus pronounced as blessed those who are meek, poor in spirit, and mourning.

Verse 14 literally reads, "Blessed is the man who is continually in fear, but the one who hardens his heart falls into trouble." Contrary to some translations (cp. NIV), the phrase "the LORD" is not present in the Hebrew. Thus, these two verses could be read to mean that whoever admits his guilt and shows remorse to the community will receive mercy from the community and that the one who fears to do wrong will stay out of trouble. Of course, one can also see a theological truth here—that those who fear God and confess their sins to Him receive mercy.

Tyranny (28:15, 16)

The tyrant is like a beast in that he is vicious (v. 15) and lacks human understanding (v. 16).

Guilt and Innocence (28:17, 18)

Like 28:13, 14, these verses contrast the misery of guilt with the freedom of a pure conscience. The description of the life of the murderer in verse 17 seems to reflect the account of the mark of Cain in Genesis 4:10–15.

Prosperity by Fair and Foul Means (28:19–27)

This passage describes various means of acquiring money; some of them are just and some are evil. Proverbs does not condemn the acquisition of possessions, but it always opposes greed (v. 20). It contrasts the building up of wealth through hard work, wise investment, and prudent use of money with all unscrupulous means of getting money. The latter category includes "get-rich-quick" schemes (v. 19), accepting bribes (v. 21), flattery (v. 23), and robbing one's parents (v. 24).

Apocalyptic literature frequently describes oppressive governments as beasts (cp. Dan. 7:1–8).

Verse 19 contrasts hard work with "empty things," get-rich-quick schemes that many indulge in. In the latter category one could include "too-good-to-be-true" investment schemes and lottery tickets. Verse 20 contrasts two attitudes. One man is faithful in doing his work and in managing his life, and the other is greedy. True riches (not necessarily financial) come to the former and are always beyond the grasp of the latter. Verse 21 deals with accepting bribes ("a piece of bread"). The point is that greed drives people to sell their souls cheaply. If verse 21 describes how greedy people end up selling out cheaply, verse 22 completes the ironic tale: Those eager for riches end up impoverished. Verse 23 focuses on flattery and how people use it to gain favor and money from the rich. The verse declares that those who are honest and respected for it are the ones who will succeed. Verse 24 describes the kind of person that Proverbs regards as especially despicable: the man who would defraud his own parents.

Verses 25–27 close this passage with three basic teachings. First, greedy people only cause trouble; true prosperity with peace comes by trusting in the Lord (v. 25). Second, no one is smart enough to attain wealth with happiness; those who submit to divine teaching, however, have true security in life (v. 26). Third, those who are generous have more financial security than those who hoard (v. 27).

- *The desire for financial security is universal;*
- *the ways of attaining it are very different.*
- *Those who succumb to greed become corrupt*
- *and often end up in poverty. Those who are*
- *prudent, hardworking, submitted to God,*
- *and generous are the ones who are really*
- *secure and happy.*

Good Government and Bad Government, Part II (28:28–29:2)

This text echoes 28:12 and makes the point that bad leadership pulls a people down into moral decay and misery while good leadership makes a people thrive. Proverbs 29:1 makes the point that the wicked will ultimately be destroyed.

Squandering Wealth and Squandering a Nation (29:3, 4)

These two proverbs relate to one another as the economy of the household relates to the economy of the nation. A corrupt son squanders the family wealth (v. 3) as surely as a corrupt ruler squanders the national resources (v. 4).

Beware of the Traps (29:5, 6)

These two proverbs focus on the metaphor of the trap that the evil man sets for his victims. Verse 6 should be rendered, "There is a snare in the iniquity of an evil man, but the righteous shout for joy and rejoice." In other words, the righteous avoid the machinations of these frauds and live in joy.

Concern for Justice (29:7)

A characteristic of those who know God is concern for the poor and their rights. Absence of this virtue is a sign that a person does not know God.

Order in the Court and in Society (29:8–11)

This text describes how evil people cause chaos and violence in society while upright persons maintain justice and peace. Verse 10 should be translated, "Bloodthirsty men hate the innocent, but the upright seek to avenge (the innocent man's) life." Understood in this way, the whole text exhibits a parallel structure:

A: Mockers make havoc but the wise restore order (v. 8).

  B: The wise have self-control; fools do not (v. 9).

A´: Violent men harm the innocent, but the upright restore justice (v. 10).

  B´: The wise have self-control; fools do not (v. 9).

The Throne Secured by Righteousness (29:12–14)

Verses 12 and 14 are similar in structure and message; both assert that a ruler who allows evil to flourish will be consumed in that evil. In the middle stands verse 13, which asserts that the Lord made both the poor and those who oppress them. The implied warning is that those who use their power to plunder the weak will face divine judgment.

Evangelicals sometimes have an instinctive reaction against focusing on the plight of the poor because of its associations with the older "social gospel" and the more recent "liberation theology." Concern for the poor, however, is at the heart of biblical justice and should never be scorned by those who maintain fidelity to the teachings of the Bible.

Discipline at Home and in the Nation (29:15–18)

These proverbs relate justice in the home to justice in society (see also 29:3, 4). Verses 15 and 17 assert the necessity of teaching and disciplining children. By contrast, verse 16 warns against a situation where the evil thrive unpunished in society and verse 18 asserts that society needs the teaching of the law and the prophets. It is not enough to have punishment (the rod in the home or the executioner in society). There must also be teaching from parents at home and from prophets and priests in society.

Controlling the Servant and Controlling the Self (29:19–22)

The word translated "vision" in verse 18 is often associated with the prophets, as in Obadiah 1. In connection with "law" in Proverbs 29:18, therefore, "vision" refers to the ministry of the prophets in bringing the word of God to the people.

These four verses set up a parallel between the need to discipline one's slaves (vv. 19, 21) and the need to discipline one's self (vv. 20, 22). The person who speaks in haste and is hot-tempered is similar to the slave who has never been taught to do his duty; both lack discipline. This passage does not imply that we should treat subordinates cruelly any more than it suggests that a person should abuse himself physically in the name of self-discipline.

The First Shall Be Last (29:23)

The reversal of fortunes described here is perhaps the origin of Jesus' teaching that the first will be last and the last first (Matt. 19:30).

A Poor Choice for a Friend (29:24)

A person who befriends a thief places himself in danger of coming under a curse. If he is called upon to testify, he cannot (either out of friendship or fear of reprisal). But in refusing to testify, he violates an oath and makes himself liable under the curse of the oath (see Lev. 5:1).

Seek Deliverance from God (29:25, 26)

It is fitting that here, near the end of the collection of Hezekiah, we read a simple summary of divine wisdom: Do not fear people or seek justice primarily from human authorities—trust God above all.

The Sum of It All (29:27)

At the very end of the Hezekiah collection we have the simplest moral lesson of all. There are two classes of people: the righteous and the evil. One must choose which path to follow.

- ■ *This summarizing book illustrates that the*
- ■ *book of Proverbs deals in general truths*
- ■ *more than in specific or exceptional cases. Of*
- ■ *course, it is true that people are complex, and*
- ■ *that even great and devout people can have*
- ■ *real character flaws. On the other hand, it is*
- ■ *certainly true that there are those who care*
- ■ *about right and wrong and about obedience*
- ■ *to God, and there are those who do not.*

THE SAYINGS OF AGUR (30:1–33)

We know nothing about Agur, son of Jakeh, but contrary to some interpreters, there is no reason to take this as a pseudonym for Solomon. Ancient Israel had many scribes and sages about whom we have little or no information. This chapter contains a series of distinct teachings on various subjects, but many of the sayings have numerical patterns and many are enigmatic in nature. The words, "an oracle," in verse 1 properly belong with what follows, 1b–6.

The Limits of Human Understanding (30:1b–6)

The opening words, "The man declares to Ithiel, to Ithiel and Ucal" (NASB) are quite perplexing. It is possible that Agur is simply giving the names of teachers from whom he has learned, but it is not clear why he would do that here. The ancient versions are very different, and this implies that the text may have been poorly transmitted. An alternative interpretation that requires little modification of the Hebrew is, "I am weary, O God, weary and exhausted." This seems to fit the context well, in which the speaker declares that he has been unable to resolve the mysteries of life.

Because humans are so limited in their ability to grasp the meaning of reality, we are doomed to remain in the dark unless God gives us light. It is the word of God that is flawless and trustworthy (v. 5). Interestingly, however, this text gives a special warning to those who "add to his [God's] words" in verse 6. This is an offense that the believer may be more prone to than the unbeliever. Often we delude ourselves with the idea that all our concepts and beliefs come directly from the Bible when in fact we have added ideas that come from tradition, from "dynamic" teachers, and from Christian subculture.

■ *Speaking with the clarity and honesty of a sage,*
■ *Agur begins by admitting he is unable to*
■ *answer many of life's deepest questions. In this*
■ *condition, he is able to embrace the truth that*
■ *God alone can give. As if to reinforce the fact*
■ *that finding truth is often difficult, many of the*
■ *sayings of chapter 30 are very enigmatic.*

A Humble Prayer (30:7–9)

What are the "two things" that he asks God to keep from him? One might think that they are (1) keep lies and deceit from me and (2) do not make me rich or poor. In his explanation, however, he deals only with the various troubles that come from poverty and from riches. It appears that lies and deceit are the qualities that characterize excessive wealth and grinding poverty. Both of these deceive; riches tell a person that he can get along without God, and poverty tells him that God does not care. Thus, the two things he wants to avoid are wealth and poverty.

The Ordinary Worker (30:10)

The modern counterparts to slave and master are the employee and boss. One should not impugn another's character before his superiors without good cause.

The Lowest Forms of Life (30:11–14)

The four types of people mentioned here are, from the perspective of wisdom, as low and detestable as human beings can become. They are (1) those who refuse to honor their parents, (2) hypocrites unaware—people who wallow in moral filth but do not understand how evil they have become, (3) the haughty, and (4) people who are violent, oppressive, and abusive. In naming the four in a list such as this, the text gives us a simple-to-memorize list of the kind of characteristics we should avoid.

Insatiable Things (30:15, 16)

This is a combination of two numerical sayings (v. 15a and vv. 15b, 16) that join to make a single saying. Note that there is a progression of two, three, and four in the text. The two "daughters" of the leech are the two suckers at either end of its body. Their names are "Give!" and

Of themselves, these four items do not give us any moral lesson. After verse 15a, however, it appears that they are metaphors for human greed. People driven by greed never get enough and never give back. Like the womb that never gives birth, these people never compensate the world for all they have taken away. Like the fire, the grave, and the land, they constantly consume.

The commandment, "Honor your father and your mother, so that you may live long in the land the LORD your God is giving you," stands behind 30:17. The point is that respect for parents is the key to learning respect for all authority and for rules in general. People who cannot live with authority or rules frequently die young due to violence, substance abuse, or carelessness. Those who honor parents can accept limits and generally live long, peaceful lives.

"Give!" ("they cry," found in the NIV, is not in the original text). It may be that in ancient Israel, "The leech has two daughters, 'Give! Give!'" was the kind of proverb an exasperated mother would use when her children were begging her for something. Verses 15b, 16 add four things that are insatiable: the grave, because it never has enough of the dead; the barren womb, because it never has enough to cause it to give birth; land, because it always soaks up more water; and fire, because it never has enough of things to burn.

The Hater of Parents (30:17)

The obvious point here is that those who do not respect parents are accursed. What is not so obvious is that the reason the eyes are plucked out and eaten by scavenger birds is that the body lies unburied. That is, this person, because he has abandoned his proper place within the family and has scorned parents, dies alone and is left unburied after a death that was probably violent.

A Riddle and a Clue (30:18–20)

In a numerical saying, the author declares that there are four things he cannot understand: an eagle in the sky, a snake on a rock, a ship on the sea, and a man with a young woman. The obvious riddle is: What do these four things have in common and why does the man find it mysterious? Interpreters have proposed many solutions, but most seem to fall flat. For example, some say that the answer is that they deal with mastery over the elements, such as how a ship masters the sea or an eagle masters the sky. But the idea that a snake masters a rock is forced and the notion that a man masters a young woman is harsh and improbable.

It is better to read verse 20 as a clue. The line, "This is the way of an adulteress," obviously parallels the four "ways" of verse 19, which implies that verse 20 is tied to verses 18, 19. The remarkable thing about the adulteress is that she is unaware of having done any wrong. In fact, she walks away from a sexual liaison with the same nonchalance that she has in finishing a meal. As far as she is concerned, the deed is over and it has no repercussions or aftermath.

In this light, it is easy to see what the four things of verse 19 have in common: they all describe activity which leaves no trail. A bird in the sky, a snake on a rock, and a ship on the sea all move on without leaving any visible wake or sign that they had been there (this was, of course, in a time before motorized boats). Thus, what astonishes the author is that a man and woman can come together for a night of sex and think that the next day they can move on without any commitment or aftereffects. Such people think that like a snake on a rock, they can have their time of sexual activity and then move on as if nothing had happened. In fact, this is a delusion. The aftereffects of emotional scarring, pregnancy, and sexually transmitted diseases are very great.

Insufferable People (30:21–23)

This numerical saying leads into a chiasmus of four items:

A: Male servant usurps his master (22a)
   B: Male fool full of food (22b)
   B′: Married woman without love (23a)
A′: Female servant usurps her mistress (23b).

The male servant of A contrasts with the female servant of A′ as the male full of food in B contrasts with the female deprived of love in B′. There is also parallelism here: A and B are both

None of us wants to be regarded by peers as out of our depth, obnoxious, or tedious to be around. The only escape from such a condition is the grace of God. He humbles us without breaking our spirits. He gives the joy and love that makes us lovable.

males, while B´ and A´ are both females. The point of the text is that there are people who make life miserable for everyone around them. A servant who suddenly has authority but lacks the training and disposition for leadership is unbearable. One might even say that the "servant" here is not necessarily a person who has had that position in life (consider Joseph, who was once a slave) but is someone who is mentally and emotionally unsuited for anything but subordination. Similarly, a "fool" who has all he wants becomes all the more obnoxious. A woman who is desperate to feel loved, no matter how much we may sympathize with her plight, is difficult to endure.

Lessons from Animals (30:24–28)

The four animals of this saying teach us lessons about succeeding despite our limitations. The ants teach us that a person doesn't have to be great and wise to have enough sense to take care of his or her basic needs. Even ants know you have to store up provisions while they are available. The coneys (v. 26; coneys are small, European rabbits) teach us that even weak things can find security if they work at finding it. Locusts tell us that we will be much stronger together if we cooperate even when there is no king standing over us giving orders. The lizard tells us that even if we are people of no significance, we can arise to high places. Coming after verses 21–23, this text tells us that our attitude is much more important than our station in life.

Royal Creatures (30:29–31)

This is a numerical saying in which the first three items, animals that are majestic, in some way explain or illustrate the fourth thing, the grandeur of a king. On the surface, it appears that these four things have nothing in common except they are somehow stately and impressive, and it is hard to see any clear moral lesson here. One could search for clues in the descriptions of the lion, the he-goat, and the rooster, but this does not appear to be a very fruitful approach. The one thing that is distinctive is that the grandeur of the three animals is intrinsic to the animals themselves; that is, it is a quality the animals possess *by nature*. In the case of the king, however, majesty is not intrinsic to the man himself but is in the army—*the followers*—who march with him. It appears that this is a riddle on leadership, and the message is this: You are nothing as a leader unless people are willing to follow you. A crown and scepter do not make for majesty; an army does.

A leader must never forget that he is nothing without followers. If people are not willing to follow your lead, it does not matter that you have the title of president, pastor, professor, general, CEO, or academic dean. Leadership is bankrupt if it depends upon pulling rank or manipulation. Even claiming that one has authority by virtue of the call of God soon wears thin if the individual does not know how to maintain a following.

If You Are Obnoxious (30:32, 33)

Sometimes the language of the Bible is lost on us; we miss the point simply because the text does not use the kind of words we would use. The opening of verse 32, "If you have been foolish in exalting yourself" (NASB), really means, "If you have been an obnoxious jerk." The warning that follows is very simple: Cover your nose, because it is very likely that someone is ready to punch you in the face! The lesson is self-evident. Do not be obnoxious unless you enjoy having people think you are an idiot and take a swing at you.

■ *The sayings of Agur are riddles on human*
■ *behavior. The general thrust of the text is*
■ *that greedy, obnoxious, and arrogant behav-*
■ *ior makes people unbearable and worthy of*
■ *all the trouble that comes to them. By con-*
■ *trast, learning a few simple lessons—so sim-*
■ *ple that even the animals could teach them to*
■ *us—leads to honor and respect.*

THE SAYINGS OF LEMUEL'S MOTHER (31:1–9)

Like Agur, Lemuel is unknown outside of this text of Proverbs, but once again there are no grounds for taking Lemuel as a pseudonym for Solomon. With a minor emendation of the Hebrew, one may translate verse 1a as, "The sayings of Lemuel, King of Massa," instead of "an oracle." Massa seems to have been a North Arabian tribe (Gen. 25:14; 1 Chron. 1:30).

Lemuel's mother has three basic teachings on good government: Do not use your power to indulge in debauchery (v. 3), stay sober (vv. 4–7), and use your authority to defend the weak (vv. 8, 9). Verses 6, 7 do not mean that it is wise to promote alcoholism in the lower classes as a means of keeping them happy. The text might be paraphrased as follows: "If strong drink has any value, it is for the impoverished and the most wretched members of the despondent; but you must not let yourself become like one of these, Lemuel." The duty of Lemuel is not to intoxicate members of society (and ultimately make their condition more hopeless than ever) but to speak up for them and defend them (vv. 8, 9).

- *The mother of Lemuel gave him lessons that*
- *apply to anyone in authority. A person must*
- *not use his or her power for self-indulgence*
- *but for the good of others. Or, as Jesus put it,*
- *the one who is first must be servant of all.*

THE GOOD WIFE (31:10–31)

The poem in praise of the good wife provides fitting closure to the book of Proverbs. After thirty chapters of sayings and warnings for the young man, teachings that emphasize how he should conduct himself, it is refreshing to end on a text that portrays a woman as strong, dedicated, and compassionate. One should not assume, however, that this is a tidbit thrown in to give some instruction to female readers. The young man is still the intended audience of the book, as the structure of this text makes clear. The poem is shaped as a large chiasmus, as follows:

A: High value of the good wife (v. 10)
   B: Husband benefited by wife (vv. 11, 12)
      C: Wife works hard (vv. 13–19)
         D: Wife gives to poor (v. 20)
            E: No fear of snow (v. 21a)
               F: Children clothed in scarlet (v. 21b)
                  G: Coverings for bed; wife wears linen (v. 22)
                     H: Public respect for husband (v. 23)
                  G': Sells garments and sashes (v. 24)
               F': Wife clothed in dignity (v.25a)
            E': No fear of future (v. 25b)
         D': Wife speaks wisdom (v. 26)
      C': Wife works hard (v. 27)
   B': Husband and children praise wife (vv. 28, 29)
A': High value of good wife (vv. 30, 31)

As the above outline demonstrates, each element of the first part of the poem has a counterpart in the second part. For example, the fact that the good wife has no fear of snow for her children (v. 21) has a parallel in the fact that she is not anxious about the future (v. 25b). She demonstrates wisdom by showing compassion to the poor in verse 20 and teaches wisdom in verse 26. The fact that the wife benefits the husband (vv. 11, 12) has a parallel in how the husband and children praise the wife (vv. 28, 29).

In a chiasmus, however, the central element is often the most important part of the text for determining the meaning and purpose of the whole. It is the pivot point for the whole passage. Here, the central text is the fact that the husband is respected in the gate (that is, among his peers, who are the other men of the city). In other words, this is a text telling the young man what kind of woman he needs to marry if he wants to live a successful, happy life and have the respect of the community.

A young person needs to look long and hard at the character of the person he or she considers marrying. Sexy looks, a winning personality, and popularity are not of themselves bad, but they are not the basis for a lifelong commitment. Few things cause as much pain and regret as marrying a person of bad morals or weak character.

This is not to say that the woman is merely an appendage for the man and has no function beyond adding to his honor. Certainly the woman here has intelligence, energy, character, and compassion; she is no accessory. Still, this is a text for a young man in that it teaches him to find a woman who will bring him joy, not misery. When the text says, "Charm is deceitful and beauty is passing" (NKJV), these words are for the benefit of the male reader, not for the good woman (who would probably regard such a line as a backhanded compliment).

When the text asks who can find a woman of high character (v. 10), it is not a cynical assertion that there are no women of such character. It means that a woman like this is the find of a lifetime. Verse 13 can actually be translated to mean that the woman works "at the pleasure of her hands." The hands are personified as taking joy in their work and going about it with purpose. Verse 15 does not necessarily mean that she personally serves breakfast to servant girls, which would be highly unusual in the ancient world, but that she supervises the beginning of the day's activities and sees to it that the girls are fed. Still, the text tells us that she takes care of the needs of her subordinates.

Verse 21 strikes readers as odd in that it is not clear why scarlet clothing would protect children against the cold. Some emend the Hebrew to read, "clothing of double layers," but this is a questionable interpretation. Probably, the idea is not that scarlet-colored garments are of themselves warm but that these are clothes of very high quality. Similarly, the linen and purple the woman wears (v. 22) show that she has good taste. Linen represents an import from Egypt and purple an import from Phoenicia; both would be expensive and stylish.

The book of Proverbs, from beginning to end, lays out the choice for the young man in terms of two ways—the way of integrity and God over against the way of folly and self-indulgence. It presents the way of wisdom in the personification of Lady Wisdom appealing to young men to learn of her. Similarly, Woman Folly—the archetypal prostitute—represents the way of evil. It is fitting, therefore, that the book should end by exhorting the young man to find not just the metaphorical Lady Wisdom but a literal, living, breathing, wise woman to share his life with.

■ *The poem in praise of the good woman con-*
■ *cludes Proverbs with the implied exhortation*
■ *that the young man will not have a successful*
■ *and joyful life without a good and godly*
■ *woman at his side. She is hard-working,*
■ *savvy with money, a good manager, compas-*
■ *sionate, and godly. She also has class. She*
■ *deserves all the praise she receives. With*
■ *such a wife, it is no wonder that the men of*
■ *the city respect her husband.*

QUESTIONS TO GUIDE YOUR STUDY

1. What kinds of people does Proverbs encourage us to avoid?
2. What one attribute do fools possess that undermines their effectiveness in life?
3. What is a sluggard and what four kinds of behaviors does he or she manifest?
4. Why is a man's choice of a wife so important?
5. List some of the skills and virtues of the woman described in Proverbs 31.